THIS OTHER EDEN

Ireland Into Film

Series editors:

Keith Hopper (text) and Gráinne Humphreys (images)

Ireland into Film is the first project in a number of planned collaborations between Cork University Press and the Film Institute of Ireland. The general aim of this publishing initiative is to increase the critical understanding of 'Irish' Film (i.e. films made in, or about, Ireland). This particular series brings together writers and scholars from the fields of Film and Literary Studies to examine notable adaptations of Irish literary texts.

Other titles available in this series:

The Dead (Kevin Barry)
December Bride (Lance Pettitt)

Forthcoming titles:

The Informer (Patrick F. Sheeran)
The Field (Cheryl Herr)
Nora (Gerardine Meaney)
The Quiet Man (Luke Gibbons)
The Butcher Boy (Colin MacCabe)

Ireland Into Film

THIS OTHER EDEN

Fidelma Farley

CORK UNIVERSITY PRESS

in association with
THE FILM INSTITUTE OF IRELAND

First published in 2001 by
Cork University Press
Cork
Ireland

British Library Cataloguing in Publication Data
A CIP catalogue record for this book is available from the British Library.

ISBN 1 85918 289 5

Typesetting by Red Barn Publishing, Skeagh, Skibbereen

Printed by ColourBooks Ltd, Baldoyle, Dublin

Ireland into Film receives financial assistance from
the Arts Council / An Chomhairle Ealaíon and the Film Institute of Ireland

To Jane, Aoileann agus Tom, le grá

CONTENTS

LIST OF ILLUSTRATIONS

Acknowledgements

Thanks to: the English Department at the University of Aberdeen for research leave to write this book; Robert Monk at the Liam O'Leary Archive in the National Library, Dublin; the staff at the library and Special Collections at the British Film Institute; Gráinne Humphreys at the Irish Film Centre for her excavation of images; Ciara O'Farrell for permission to consult her PhD thesis; Aoileann Farley for help with references; Shane Murphy; Keith Hopper for his patience and comments on the text; the Carnegie Trust for the Universities of Scotland for its contribution towards research and travel expenses; John McMahon for help with tapes; Margaret Brindley for help with various computer problems.

The editors would also like to thank Sheila Pratschke, Lar Joye, Michael Davitt, Luke Dodd, Dennis Kennedy, Kevin Rockett, Ellen Hazelkorn, Seán Ryder, St Cross College (Oxford), the School of Irish Studies Foundation and the Arts Council of Ireland.

The publishers wish to thank the Irish Architectural Archive for permission to reproduce Plate 15, Ardmore Studios for Plate 2, the National Theatre of Ireland for Plate 14, and the BBC for all other plates reproduced herein.

INTRODUCTION

Although the play on which *This Other Eden*[1] was based was very popular when it was performed in 1953, and although the film itself, released six years later, achieved a modest commercial and critical success, both play and film have since faded into relative obscurity.[2] The film was given a retrospective screening at the Irish Film Centre and was shown on RTÉ some years ago, but, in general, it is known only to specialists in Irish cinema and drama. At first glance, the reasons for this seem to be evident. The film is a competently made comedy but lacks a distinctive cinematic style and major stars. Its director, Muriel Box, has until recently been consigned to a footnote in British cinema history as an interesting but mediocre director. Likewise, Louis D'Alton, author of the original play, is a minor figure in the pantheon of Irish dramatists, his plays rarely performed now.

However, there is a range of reasons why *This Other Eden* deserves to be rescued from its relative neglect, and it is hoped that this piece will go some way towards bringing it to the attention of a wider audience. Firstly, the film is the most accomplished of the adaptations of Abbey plays produced at Ardmore Studios in Bray between 1958 and 1960. The intention behind the establishment of Ireland's first purpose-built film studio, and the Abbey adaptations produced there, was to encourage the growth of an indigenous film industry. Although the development of a national cinema which would critically explore and reflect upon Ireland was not the aim of those behind Ardmore Studios, who envisaged an American and, to a lesser extent, a British target audience for their films, *This Other Eden*'s relevance is primarily to an Irish audience. The device of the visiting Englishman is used not to present Ireland as a spectacle for foreign eyes but to present Ireland to the Irish themselves. The film

Plate 1. Original publicity poster for This Other Eden.

makes a mockery of romanticized constructions of Ireland by the English, but the principal target of its satire is Irish romanticization of Ireland and Irish identity. *This Other Eden* critiques 1950s Ireland by making the audience laugh at themselves and the beliefs they take for granted.

Secondly, *This Other Eden* is of interest because it provides an opportunity to assess the place of the film in the work of its English director, Muriel Box the first woman to direct an Irish feature film. Box's prolific output during the 1940s and 1950s is an extraordinary achievement for a woman working in an industry which was at best indifferent and at worst actively hostile to female directors. Although the increase in academic interest in British cinema history and in women directors has focused attention on Box in recent years, critical accounts of her work either fail to mention *This Other Eden* or give it only a passing mention.

An appraisal of the film also provides an opportunity to assess D'Alton's play, a reworking and updating of Shaw's *John Bull's Other Island* (1904), and to put it in the context of the work of this prolific and popular playwright. Writing at a time of social and political conservatism, and during a stagnant period at the Abbey Theatre, D'Alton's plays skilfully negotiate a path between social critique and audience popularity. Although both Box and D'Alton had strong political views, both chose to express their views in popular formats which would simultaneously educate and entertain the audience. *This Other Eden*, play and film, is a particularly successful example of their skill in this respect.

Finally, the film, particularly, is a remarkably early treatment of the concerns which would exercise Irish film-makers from the 1970s onwards. Through its exploration of the legacy of the past, it addresses a wide range of issues, including emigration, the power and wealth of the Church, the reverence of nationalist martyrs, illegitimacy and anti-English hostility. It debunks essentialist notions of national identity by juxtaposing the 'fiction' of authentic national identity with the 'facts' of contemporary Ireland. It would take another twenty years before these issues were taken up by Irish film-makers in films characterized by anger and a desire to confront Irish audiences with the failures of contemporary Ireland.

Produced in a decade of moral, social and political conservatism, and with an eye to commercial success, *This Other Eden* subsumes its anger into satire, and into the weary resignation of one of its principal characters, the cynical Devereaux. However, that it was made at all is evidence of the shifts taking place in the late 1950s away from the insularity and isolationism of the 1930s and 1940s, and the film's narrative echoes in utopian fashion this shift from an obsession with the past to an engagement with the future.

The use of comedy as critique is a double-edged sword: it allows for the expression of views which may be generally unacceptable or provocative, but it also allows the audience to dismiss them as 'just comedy'. *This Other Eden*'s use of comedy facilitates the voicing of dissatisfaction with contemporary Irish society in a 'safe' way, the laughter it produces softening the impact of its critical thrusts. Nonetheless, by focussing on the victims of the idealized Ireland constructed by the discourses of cultural nationalism and condemning those who have a vested interest in maintaining this idealized national self-image, both play and film take complacent assumptions of national difference and superiority to task.

1

SYNOPSIS OF THE FILM

The film begins with a prologue, set during the War of Independence. It is night-time, and Mick Devereaux (Peadar Lamb) and Commandant Jack Carberry (Gerald Sullivan) are on their way to meet a British Army officer with a view to negotiating a cease-fire. Unknown to them, Black and Tans are placing themselves in hiding at the meeting place. When Devereaux and Carberry arrive at the apparently deserted road, Carberry walks down the road and is fired upon by the hidden soldiers, who escape quickly once they have shot him. Devereaux rushes from the car to his friend and kneels beside him as Carberry asks Devereaux, just before he dies, to 'see to everything'.

The credit sequence follows, with the credits appearing over a tracking shot moving alongside a large house and grounds, with horses in the foreground. The scene then fades to a long shot of a sunny country road. A postman (Philip O'Flynn) alights from his bicycle beside a stone cross, lights a cigarette and throws away the match. The camera moves to a close-up of the inscription at the base of the cross, which commemorates the spot where Carberry was killed. The postman cycles into Ballymorgan, to the Central Hotel, and enters the hotel bar. Pat Tweedy (Milo O'Shea) serves him a drink and they discuss the hotel owner, McRoarty, described by the postman as a 'gombeen' man. McRoarty (Geoffrey Golden) enters and tells Pat that he will be spending the afternoon at a meeting of the Carberry Memorial Committee, and that his daughter Maire will be arriving by train that afternoon, having returned from England.

At Heuston Station in Dublin, we see Maire (Audrey Dalton) arriving by taxi and entering the station. Her taxi is closely followed by another, from which Crispin Brown (Leslie Phillips) emerges, speaking heavily accented Irish to the uncomprehending driver. Crispin catches the train just as it is leaving the station, getting into the carriage occupied by Maire. A conversation between them ensues, during which there is some confusion over Maire's nationality: Crispin initially thinks she is English and implores her to be mindful of England's past treatment of Ireland. When she tells him that she is in fact Irish, Crispin tells her that he too wishes to become Irish and hopes to settle in Ballymorgan.

Back in Ballymorgan, McRoarty is in the office of the *Ballymorgan Eagle* with its editor, Mick Devereaux (Niall MacGinnis). We learn that a large house, Kilcarrig, is shortly to be auctioned and that the nuns intend to buy it. McRoarty has learned that an Englishman is also interested, but Devereaux is of the opinion that the Englishman has no chance of buying Kilcarrig if the nuns want it. The sound of a truck screeching to a halt brings the two men to the window. They look down at the town square where the preparations for the erection of a statue of Carberry are taking place. Clannery (Harry Brophy) enters the office, excited about the arrival of the statue, but, disgruntled by Devereaux's lack of enthusiasm, he leaves again. Devereaux mentions to McRoarty that Conor Heaphy is returning from college that afternoon.

The action cuts to Conor (Norman Rodway) waiting at Castlefinbar train station. When the train arrives, Maire greets Conor warmly and he joins her and Crispin in the dining-car.

In Ballymorgan, Canon Moyle (Hilton Edwards) is in conference with the Mother Superior (Ria Mooney), who tells the Canon that she expects him to use his influence to ensure that the nuns get Kilcarrig at a reasonable price. In the meantime, McNeely, the local TD (Paul Farrell), Sergeant Crilly (Eddie Golden) and Devereaux are shown into the adjoining room, shortly followed by McRoarty. Sergeant Crilly asks McNeely what kind of man Carberry was. McNeely's reverential description of Carberry as a patriot martyr is greeted with cynicism by Devereaux. The Canon shows the men into his office and reiterates his opposition to the Carberry statue, claiming that he cannot endorse any celebration of Carberry.

The action then cuts between shots of a horse and trap containing Maire, Crispin and Conor, and Devereaux, McNeely, McRoarty and Pat in the hotel bar. Pat maintains that McRoarty must have been mistaken about Crispin Brown being English, as he had rung the hotel and was anxious to know if Irish was spoken in the area. They conclude that Crispin must be from Dublin. Clannery enters, in a fury because an Englishman is about to 'invade the area', as he puts it. He announces that he will strongly resist the Englishman and is not appeased by McRoarty's reassurance that Crispin is from Dublin. The horse and trap passes by Kilcarrig, and the jarvey (Derry Power) tells Crispin that it had been owned by an English colonel, who, it is rumoured, was the man who led Carberry into the ambush.

They arrive at the hotel and Maire introduces Crispin to the assembled company, who are astonished and amused by Crispin's attempts to speak Irish to them. When Conor enters, there is a palpable air of embarrassment, which Conor notes and it puzzles him. McRoarty watches a friendly exchange between Maire and Conor with displeasure. Pat takes Crispin to his room, where more comic confusion follows about Crispin's nationality. Talking about Carberry, Pat tells Crispin that, when Carberry lay dying, the English colonel kicked him savagely. Crispin reacts angrily, denying the veracity of the story, but recovers himself when he notices Pat's bemusement.

Maire and her father have tea together at the hotel, and McRoarty asks her what relations are between her and Conor. He tells Maire that Conor is illegitimate, and is shocked by Maire's calm reaction to the news. She assures him that she and Conor are not in love, but that, if they were, his illegitimacy would make no difference to her. McRoarty reveals that he had sent Maire to England to prevent her forming a relationship with Conor.

McNeely shows Crispin around Kilcarrig, with which Crispin is delighted. McNeely assures him that, although the nuns want Kilcarrig, there may be a means to work things out to everyone's satisfaction.

In the hotel bar, Clannery is holding forth to McRoarty and the Canon about Crispin, when Crispin and McNeely enter. Clannery approaches Crispin, telling him of his hatred of all things English, and is disconcerted by Crispin's approval of his position. The rest, however, are embarrassed by Clannery's outburst and ask Crispin not to take any notice of him.

Maire and Conor enter the parish house and Conor asks to see the Canon alone. He tells the Canon of his desire to become a priest. The Canon is hesitant, advising Conor to speak to his guardian, Devereaux, before making any decisions. As Maire and Conor leave the parish house, they are seen by the jarvey, driving past on the horse and trap. When he imparts this information to the postman and the owner of Flaherty's pub (Isobel Couser), they surmise that Conor and Maire are engaged. Conor and Maire enter the pub and Conor overhears the two men laughing about the embarrassment that Conor's arrival must be causing the Carberry Memorial Committee. Conor rushes out of the pub and goes to the newspaper office to confront Devereaux. Although Devereaux is at first circumspect, he eventually tells Conor that he is the illegitimate son of Jack Carberry. Conor leaves, announcing angrily that, as he is a Carberry, he is going to make history.

We cut to a street scene, with crowds lining the streets watching a pipe band marching. In the hotel bar, Clannery mentions the suspicion surrounding the English colonel's involvement in Carberry's death, which is again hotly denied by Crispin. Devereaux tells Crispin that he, too, is suspected of the murder of Carberry, because he was the last man to see him alive, or because he was jealous of him. Sergeant Crilly enters the bar, telling the men that their presence is needed on the platform, as the unveiling of the statue is about to take place.

While McNeely gives his speech about Carberry, prior to unveiling the statue, Conor pushes his way through the crowd and stands ostentatiously in front of the covered statue. As McNeely speaks of Carberry's 'hatred of shams and lies', Devereaux, Clannery and the Canon look anxiously at Conor. Conor leaves just before Devereaux unveils the statue, whose abstract, modern design causes consternation and amusement among the crowd. Crispin loudly and angrily criticizes the statue, saying it should be destroyed.

Later that evening, McRoarty and Devereaux are in the newspaper office looking over the completed special edition of the paper dedicated to the Carberry commemoration. As they walk along the street towards the hotel, Conor sees them and hides. He crosses the square and stands in front of the statue, looking at the inscription, which reads 'In battle fearless, in life unsullied, he died in the bright flower of manhood for Ireland'.

In the pub, the jarvey reads aloud a piece in the *Ballymorgan Eagle* by Crispin denouncing the statue. The general opinion, voiced by the postman, is that the statue is indeed an atrocity, but that it is no business of Crispin's to criticize it.

Back in the hotel, Crispin asks Maire if he can speak to her privately. He tells her that he is almost certain that he will succeed in buying Kilcarrig and then goes on to speak angrily about the statue, saying that it is unworthy of Carberry. When Maire replies that she thinks that Carberry himself would find the statue amusing, Crispin commends her intelligence and, as if out of the blue, proposes to her. Maire declines, saying that she could never live in Ballymorgan – even though she hated Birmingham, Ballymorgan makes her despair.

Crispin insists that he will continue to ask her to marry him, and that he is determined to get Kilcarrig.

When Crispin enters the hotel bar, a conflict arising from a mutual misunderstanding ensues between himself and Clannery. Clannery thinks that Crispin's hatred of the statue is the result of a hatred for Carberry, and Crispin's repeated statement that the statue should be destroyed infuriates him, though it amuses everyone else in the room. Crispin is advised by McRoarty, Devereaux and Pat to keep quiet for his own safety.

In a long shot of the square, we see the statue exploding, having been blown up. Rapid editing shows people's shocked reaction in the pub and hotel bar, people running to the statue in the square, windows being opened. After a second explosion, the crowd in front of the statue remember Crispin's announcements that the statue should be destroyed, and the jarvey exhorts the crowd to seek him out.

In the hotel bar, Sergeant Crilly warns the irate Clannery not to obstruct his investigations. Clannery responds by accusing Crispin, who has just walked into the bar, of having blown up the statue. Crispin denies the accusation, but Clannery is not satisfied. He remarks on the similarity between Crispin and the English colonel, whereupon Crispin reveals that the colonel was his father, and that his father had always regretted Carberry's assassination. Devereaux recalls that Crispin's father resigned his post in sympathy with the IRA.

The sound of the angry crowd can be heard outside the hotel, and Crispin is told to hide. However, he insists on going out to the balcony and addressing the crowd. At first the crowd is hostile, but Crispin gains sympathy by his praise of Carberry and of Ireland, and by promising to pay for a new statue. In the meantime, Conor has entered and tries to go out to the balcony to tell the crowd that it is he who has blown up Carberry's statue to reveal who he is. Maire tells him that everyone in Ballymorgan already knows. A struggle ensues between Conor and Devereaux which ends with Devereaux punching Conor and knocking him out.

The crowd having dispersed, Crispin comes back into the hotel room, pleased with the result of his speech. Conor tells him that he was responsible, and Crispin congratulates him heartily. In the bar, Clannery despairs that he must apologize to Crispin, but now suspects that it is Devereaux who is responsible for the destruction of the statue. Conor goes to the bar, tells Clannery, McNeely and McRoarty what he has done and, to everyone's horror, insists that he will give himself up and stand trial so that the whole situation will be made public. Devereaux asks to speak to him privately first. He tells Conor that his mother was his, Devereaux's, sister, who met Carberry when he was on the run and sheltered him. They planned to marry, but Conor's mother died in childbirth and then Carberry was killed. Conor is still angry, until Devereaux accuses him of being self-righteous and unforgiving, qualities unsuitable for a priest.

In the bar, Maire explains the situation to Crispin. Crispin then reveals to the shocked company that he, too, is illegitimate. Clannery and McNeely are doubly shocked when it emerges that Crispin's mother was Irish, but are slightly appeased when they learn that she was a Protestant. Maire, however, is delighted by the story, much to her father's annoyance. He announces that he will make a match for her and have her married within a month. He then receives a phone call from a journalist who is coming to Ballymorgan to investigate the destruction of the statue and the ensuing riot.

The journalist, MacPherson (Bill Foley), arrives with photographers, telling them to photograph the remains of the statue, especially the part of the inscription which reads 'in life unsullied'. He goes to the *Eagle* office and confronts Devereaux, McNeely, Sergeant Crilly and Clannery, all of whom deny that there was a riot and that Conor was involved.

Conor is with the Canon, who reproves him for his actions, but admits that he is pleased that the statue is gone. He says that, if Conor has a true vocation, he can find some way for him to fulfil it.

In the newspaper office, MacPherson asks what part Crispin played in the affair. Devereaux denies Crispin's involvement, saying that he is currently engaged in 'a life and death struggle with the nuns'.

The action cuts to Crispin, the Canon, the Mother Superior and Sister Katherine (Maire Conmee) in the Canon's office. The nuns have bought Kilcarrig for £10,000 and, after some negotiation, Crispin buys it from them for £25,000.

Back in the *Eagle* office, Clannery 'confesses' to having left some sticks of explosive near the statue when it was being erected, which must have been ignited by a faulty electric cable. MacPherson leaves and, when McNeely congratulates Clannery on his cleverness, Clannery attributes it to his English mother.

At the hotel, McRoarty encounters Pat carrying Maire's suitcase. Pat informs him that Maire is returning to England. Crispin walks into the bar as Maire and McRoarty are arguing. Maire asks Crispin if he still wants to marry her and, when he says he does, informs him that he should ask her father for a substantial dowry. Devereaux, Clannery and McNeely enter during the negotiations and are amused to witness Crispin attain a sizeable dowry from McRoarty. Devereaux notes that 'the English in Ireland are more Irish than the Irish themselves'.

The final scene of the film shows Maire and Crispin walking hand in hand towards Kilcarrig.

2

ARDMORE STUDIOS

This Other Eden was one of a group of Irish films made at Ardmore Studios in Bray, County Wicklow, which had been officially opened in 1958, the year before the release of the film. One of the major obstacles to the growth of an indigenous film industry in Ireland was the lack of production facilities available to film-makers. With the notable exception of the Film Company of Ireland, which made approximately twenty-five films between 1916 and 1920, few Irish film companies survived beyond the production of a handful of films. The aim of the establishment of Ardmore Studios in the mid-1950s was to provide modern production facilities in a permanent base, which would facilitate the growth of an Irish film industry.

In 1955, Emmet Dalton, who had worked for Paramount and then for Goldwyn in Britain, returned to Ireland and teamed up with Louis Elliman, then Rank's representative for Ireland, to enter into film production in Ireland, with the eventual aim of establishing a film studio. The following year, Dalton and Elliman approached Ernest Blythe, chairman of the Abbey Theatre, with a view to filming adaptations of Abbey plays, using Abbey players.

Dublin Theatre and Television Productions was formed with Dalton, Elliman, Blythe and playwright and Abbey Theatre director, Lennox Robinson. The company began securing filming rights for Abbey plays. *Professor Tim*,[3] based on the play by George Shiels (first performed 1925), was the first film to start production. Produced at Nettlefield Studios in England and filmed on location in Ireland, it was perceived by the company as a pilot film to test the viability of setting up a film studio to enable the production of films in Ireland. Press reports at the time quote Elliman's announcement that plans for establishing a film studio were under way and expected to be near

Plate 2. Ardmore Studios.

completion within a year. The modest success of *Professor Tim* and the following film, *Boyd's Shop*,[4] gave impetus to the plan. With government aid, Elliman and Dalton bought Ardmore, a large house with extensive grounds near Bray in County Wicklow, and set about transforming it into a fully equipped studio. The large grounds could be used for shooting exterior scenes, and its proximity to Dublin lessened the delay in the transportation of film for processing to London (it was intended that a laboratory for processing film would be added at a later date).

The studios were officially opened in May 1958 by Seán Lemass, then Minister for Industry and Commerce, while *Home is the Hero*,[5] based on Walter Macken's play, was being filmed. Press reports of the event lay great emphasis on the sophistication of the technology at Ardmore (Mitchell-BNC cameras, Westrex magnetic sound-recording system, Mole-Richardson lighting system, Houston camera cranes) and its size, with four self-contained stages and a water-tank for filming underwater scenes. There were, however, no processing or re-recording facilities on site, with the result that rushes would have to be flown to London at the end of each day, processed at a laboratory and returned the following afternoon, and that post-recording would also have to be done at a London studio.

Another recurrent feature of reports on the studios was the stress laid on the fact that the studios would be manned by Irish personnel. A piece in the *Sunday Independent* on the filming of *Professor Tim* and the plans to erect a studio states that, 'This is the first absolutely all-Irish venture in the cinema industry, with Irish personnel, 100 per cent Irish capital and no connection, even indirectly, with any British or American film organization.'[6] In a similar vein, a later report on the studios by Julia Monks in the *Irish Press* states that, 'Ardmore Studios is primarily an Irish industry, financed with Irish capital; and its proud intention is to employ Irish technicians and Irish labour wherever humanly possible.'[7] However, Monks adds:

> But film-making is so highly skilled in almost every one of its many branches, needing years of specialized training, that it will obviously be quite a while before there will be anything like a 100 per cent Irish staff at Ardmore. (To expedite this, a training-school for Irish would-be technicians is to be established.)[8]

Unfortunately, these optimistic reports were to be proved wrong. The training school was never established, and the vast majority of staff employed at Ardmore, on both Irish and foreign productions, was British. Part of the reason for this was that Ardmore management was eager to attract foreign production companies. The Irish Film Finance Corporation was formed as a subsidiary to the Industrial Credit Company to provide financial assistance to film companies wishing to use Ardmore's facilities, but no conditions were made to ensure preference for Irish film companies, nor that productions had to employ a certain quota of Irish staff. In addition, an agreement was made with the British film technicians' union, ACTT (Association of Cine and Television Technicians), that only ACTT technicians would be employed. This led to prolonged labour disputes with the Irish electrician's union, ETU(I), between 1962 and 1964, and it was telling that the striking workers were not supported by Ardmore management. As Kevin Rockett comments:

> One can see . . . the extent to which Ardmore had become part of the British film industry in the determination – and the power – of the British unions to close production there if it threatened to leave their orbit . . . No other body of Irish film technicians [apart from electricians] could get a foothold in Ardmore from which to challenge the British monopoly.[9]

As a result, the vast majority of technical staff working on both Irish and non-Irish productions were British. Irish technical staff were thus excluded from employment opportunities and from gaining valuable experience working on larger productions.

In addition, the Irish productions made at Ardmore Studios were intended to appeal primarily to American and British audiences. From the outset, the target audience of Ardmore productions was an international one. The film adaptations of Abbey plays were intended to be shown on American television, and to get a cinema release afterwards as second features. Monks' *Irish Press* article remarks on their intended function as marketing devices to attract tourists:

> All have humour and hilarity, and will depict the less sombre side of Irish life. They will, in fact, be in the Abbey tradition as established by Mr Ernest Blythe; and no doubt both Cinema and TV audiences throughout the world – especially the US – will find them entertainingly 'Irish' and pencil in Ireland as a 'must' for their next summer holiday.[10]

This drive towards the international market was stressed by Seán Lemass in his speech at the opening of the studios, in which he announced that Ardmore productions would be aimed predominantly at the export market. Thus the Irish film industry envisaged by those involved in Ardmore was one which was profit-oriented: the overriding criterion was the commercial, rather than the artistic or critical, success of the films produced.

As Rockett comments, however, even in this, Ardmore Studios were an 'abject failure',[11] going into receivership in 1963, a mere four years after its opening, and changing hands on average every four or five years. Given Ardmore Studios' dependence on the British film industry, Ardmore management was particularly short-sighted in not having a distribution wing. With the abolition in 1948 of the quota system, whereby British distributors were required to distribute a certain percentage of British films, the balance of power within the British Film industry shifted to the distribution companies. Ardmore films, financed in part by the Irish Film Finance Corporation, were required to have a distribution guarantee, and unconnected Irish producers had little chance of getting a distribution guarantee from British companies.[12] Although Ardmore Studios did succeed in attracting a number of large-scale foreign productions, it was ultimately an ill-starred venture which never succeeded in its aim of providing a base upon which to build a flourishing Irish film industry. Ardmore has since been severely critiqued for its policies, with Fergus Linehan going so far as to argue in the *Irish Times* in 1973 that, 'in the 15 years of its existence, Ardmore Studios have undoubtedly been one of the major factors militating against the setting up of an Irish film industry . . . it is time to forget it vis à vis an Irish film industry'.[13] In the same piece, Linehan calls for a financing body which will fund low-budget films, employing Irish personnel and contributing to Irish cultural and critical activity. This demand was being made from the mid-1960s by other Irish film-makers and critics, most notably Louis Marcus. As a result of their efforts, the Irish Film Board was set up in 1980, with cultural and aesthetic relevance as criteria for funding as well as commercial concerns.

Emmet Dalton and his associates produced nine films in all between 1957 and 1962, six of them based on Abbey plays, and all except one produced by Emmet Dalton's production company, Emmet Dalton Productions: *Professor Tim, Sally's Irish Rogue*,[14] *The Big Birthday*,[15] *Home is the Hero, This Other Eden, Lies My Father Told Me*,[16] *The Webster Boy*[17] and *The Devil's Agent*.[18] Abbey actors were used in all of the films, particularly Geoffrey Golden (McRoarty in *This Other Eden*) and Harry Brogan (Clannery), and Patrick Kirwan and Blanaid Irvine were regularly used as scriptwriters. However, Abbey actors rarely took the main roles: the commercial imperative of Ardmore required actors recognizable to the film-going public, even if the actors were not major stars. Thus Julie Harris stars in *Sally's Irish Rogue*, Barry Fitzgerald in *The Big Birthday*, David Farrar and Elizabeth Sellars in *The Webster Boy* and Christopher Lee in *The Devil's Agent*. Despite their modest commercial success, the films were charged with being too stagebound, a feature which may partly be attributed to poor adaptations of original plays, and partly to the directors, all of whom were, like Muriel Box, respected within the British film industry but regarded as primarily businesslike directors, not noted for stylistic flair. Indeed, on the evidence of Box's account of the tight schedule provided for production, described below, it seems as though there was little room for anything other than an efficient and practical approach in order to complete within schedule.

Dublin Film and Television Productions considered for production four of Louis D'Alton's plays, *The Devil a Saint Would Be, Lover's Meeting, They Got What They Wanted* and *This Other Eden. They Got What They Wanted* was initially preferred, but it had already been made into a film, *Talk of Million*,[19] so *This Other Eden* was chosen instead.[20]

Another factor, noted by Kevin Rockett, that may have influenced the choice of *This Other Eden* is the similarity between Emmet Dalton and the character of Devereaux.[21] Dalton, who had been an active member of the Volunteers prior to the outbreak of

World War I, fought with the British Army in the Irish Brigade, rising to the rank of captain. In 1919, he re-joined the Volunteers and became one of Michael Collins' closest and most trusted of colleagues, partaking in the attempted rescue of Seán MacEoin from Mountjoy Jail, becoming Director of Training and accompanying Collins to London during the Treaty negotiations as a military adviser and as Liaison Officer. During the Civil War, Dalton was the pro-Treaty commanding officer of the Cork area. Although he had forcefully objected, according to Tim Pat Coogan, to Collins making a tour of inspection of the area, he accompanied Collins on the final day of his fateful tour on 22 August 1922.[22] Evidence seems to indicate that one of Collins' intentions in going to Cork was to meet with some of the IRA leaders with a view to discussing an end to hostilities.[23] Dalton was in the back seat of the open touring car with Collins when the party was ambushed at Béal na mBláth. When the first shots were fired, Dalton instructed the driver to increase his speed, but Collins insisted that the driver stop.[24] According to Dalton's account of the event, published a year later, he heard Collins cry out to him that he'd been shot. Dalton and Commandant O'Connell rushed to Collins, O'Connell dragging him behind the armoured car under covering fire from Dalton. O'Connell said an act of contrition to Collins just before he died. Dalton continues:

> How can I describe the feelings that were mine in that bleak hour, kneeling in the mud of a country road not twelve miles from Clonakilty, with the still, bleeding head of the Idol of Ireland resting on my arm. My heart was broken, my mind was numbed. I was all unconscious of the bullets that still whistled and ripped the ground beside me.[25]

Despite the strong affection, even devotion, to Collins that Dalton's account exudes, he was suspected of complicity in Collins' death in some of the many speculations around what remains one of the unsolved mysteries of Irish history. Criticism was levelled against him for not having provided adequate security for Collins on the day of the assassination and for being drunk, and his time in the British Army was grounds for suspicion that he was acting on behalf of the British secret service. Dalton later resigned from the Free State Army in protest against the introduction of a new law permitting the courtmarshalling and execution of republican prisoners. He subsequently worked as Clerk of the Seanad and then in a variety of jobs before becoming involved in the film industry in Britain.[26] Box's diaries describe a conversation she had with Dalton during the shooting of *This Other Eden*, where he talked of the deaths of his wife, mother and eldest son a few years previously. Box concludes that 'he seems a very lonely man.'[27]

The character of the cynical and weary Devereaux has clear echoes of Emmet Dalton. Devereaux was a close friend of Jack Carberry (loosely based on Michael Collins), who was with him on the night he was ambushed and killed. Carberry, like Collins, was intent upon entering negotiations to end the war. Devereaux, like Dalton, is suspected of complicity in Carberry's death and has become worn down by his own disillusionment and by the largely unspoken accusations which have dogged him. Rockett also notes that there is a parallel between Crispin's father's resignation from the British Army and Dalton's resignation from the Free State Army, both undertaken as acts of principled protest.[28]

As a founding member of Dublin Film and Television Productions, Dalton would almost certainly have taken part in the selection of *This Other Eden* for filming. It was his company, Emmet Dalton Productions, which produced the film and, although Alec Snowden is the credited producer, Box's diaries show that Dalton was involved in the preparations and production of the film. In addition, it was presumably through Dalton's influence that his own daughter, Audrey, at the time quite a well-known actor in Hollywood, plays Maire McRoarty. Taking the similarities of D'Alton and Devereaux into account, the addition to the film of the prologue concerning the assassination of Carberry is relevant. In Louis D'Alton's play, the circumstances surrounding Carberry's death are not specified: we know only that Devereaux was the last person to see Carberry alive and that he was suspected of having a hand in his death, as was the English officer in command of the area, who is later revealed to be Roger Crispin (the film makes Crispin the son of the officer). Thus the play leaves as a mystery the identity of Carberry's killer. The details in the prologue to the film make the link between Carberry and Collins, and thus between Devereaux and Dalton, more specific. Moving the setting from the Civil War to the War of Independence,[29] the prologue begins with Carberry and Devereaux discussing Carberry's forthcoming meeting with a British Army officer, the aim of which is to negotiate an end to the war, but Carberry is shot and killed by Black and Tan soldiers on his way to the meeting point. Devereaux cradles Carberry's head as he dies, as Dalton had held Collins.[30] The film unlike the play identifies Carberry's killers, (although it never clarifies under whose orders the soldiers were acting), exonerates Devereaux from any complicity in Carberry's death.

The prologue was initially written by the film's scriptwriters, Patrick Kirwan and Blanaid Irvine. It is possible that the renewal of speculation around Collins' death that arose from the publication of Rex Taylor's biography of Michael Collins in 1958,[31] the year in which the script was written, may have influenced the strengthening of the link between Carberry and Collins and Devereaux and Dalton in the film. The prologue seems to have gone through several rewrites, by Box as well as Kirwan and Irvine. Box comments in her diary:

> Re-wrote the prologue, three pages of foolscap typescript in the dining-room of pub at Wicklow while they shot scenes in the street outside. It's better but not 100% good unless one has good artists and fine night camera work. Emmet Dalton preferred it to Pat's new version anyway.[32]

Without further evidence, one can only speculate on the extent of Dalton's personal investment in, and influence on, *This Other Eden*. Nonetheless, knowledge of Dalton's history and his role in producing the film produces an interpretative shift in relation to Devereaux's character. In Louis D'Alton's play, Devereaux functions primarily as a mouthpiece for the disaffected playwright. In the film, Devereaux can be read as the means through which Emmet Dalton revisited a traumatic past and its legacy, 'an attempt to redress, if not rewrite, history'.[33]

3

MURIEL BOX

Muriel Box (1905–91) remains to this day the most prolific of British female directors, despite the fact that she did not begin directing until she was in her forties. She directed fourteen films between 1949 and 1964 and wrote scripts for twenty-one feature films in all, many of them with her husband, producer Sydney Box. During her directing career, she was generally regarded as nothing more than a competent director of 'women's films'. A reviewer in *Sight and Sound* commented in 1958 that, 'her . . . films are for the most part "women's pictures" . . . They are part of the magazine fiction of the screen – and no less competently organized than most magazine fiction.'[34] Since the 1970s, however, her work has undergone fairly substantial critical revision. Of particular interest is the fact that Box and Wendy Toye were the only female directors working consistently within the British film industry in the 1950s, which Sue Harper attributes to 'the bloody-mindedness of the former and the sheer insouciance of the latter'.[35] Unlike Toye, Box had feminist and socialist convictions, and critical

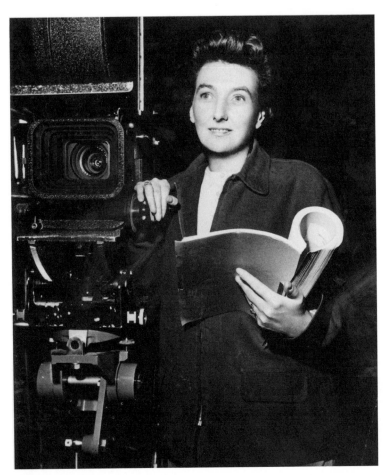

Plate 3.   Muriel Box.

revisions of her films note the ways in which Box subtly inscribed her popular, generic films with her own politics and interests.

Box continually encountered opposition and hostility as a female director, from producers, distributors and from actors, though she claimed in an interview with Brian MacFarlane that she had never experienced any difficulties with technical crews.[36] In the same interview, in response to a question about the difficulties of being a woman director, Box maintained that 'they [the industry generally] were prejudiced from the start . . . they elbowed you out'.[37] Nonetheless, Box's own determination, the popular success of the majority of her films and, undoubtedly, the support of her husband Sydney, a respected producer, sustained her directorial career until the mid-1960s.

Box's entry into the film industry was as a typist at British Instructional Films, and she graduated to personal assistant to such directors as Michael Powell and Anthony Asquith, and then to reading and editing scripts. She also began to write plays, mainly for amateur drama groups, containing strong roles for women, as parts for women were much in demand. Caroline Mertz notes that Box's experience as a playwright gave her crucial training for the scriptwriting and directing she would do later, for example in character and narrative construction and in gauging popular taste.[38]

Sydney set up Verity Films in 1939 to produce instructional and propaganda films, and Muriel was involved in film production there at every level. Unlike the documentary ethos espoused by Grierson et al, the films made at Verity used professional actors, had relatively developed narratives and aimed to entertain as much as educate. It may be through the films they made for Verity that Muriel and Sydney developed what Murphy calls the 'Box identity',[39] that is, contemporary films about ordinary people.

The enormous success of *The Seventh Veil*[40] – Muriel and Sydney won an Oscar for the script – was instrumental in Sydney being asked to head Gainsborough Studios in 1946, which at the time were renowned for their costume melodramas. Muriel was script editor and Betty Box, Sydney's sister, was a producer there. The Boxes changed the output of Gainsborough, preferring more realist films over the historical melodramas that had been so popular in the 1940s, particularly with female audiences. Although Mertz laments the fact that Muriel did not begin directing with Gainsborough in the 1940s, when its films contained strong female roles and appealed primarily to female audiences, looking at Muriel's films in the 1950s, both those she scripted and those she directed, it is clear that her preference for contemporary settings and issues and her penchant for realism are at odds with the flamboyant style and disregard for historical accuracy that characterized the Gainsborough melodramas.

It was when Muriel was required to re-shoot scenes for *The Lost People* in 1949 that her directing career began, though she continued to write scripts until the late 1950s.[41] Box's films lack stylistic flair: in terms of direction, they are competent, without distinguishing visual or formal features. Her films range across genres and themes, a reflection not just of the range of her interests but also of the British film industry in the 1950s, which, in the face of competition from Hollywood and the lifting in 1948 of the quota system, was aimed primarily at achieving audience popularity. The fourteen films directed by Box address topics as varied as the daily work of policewomen (*Street Corner*),[42] teenage promiscuity (*Too Young to Love*),[43] marriage (*Simon and Laura*)[44] and conflict between the state and the family (*The Happy Family*),[45] and inhabit various genres, such as comedy, thriller and social drama. What is consistent in her films is the foregrounding of women's roles, which may be one of the reasons why several of the films directed and/or scripted by Box experienced difficulties with the censors, and sometimes with producers and distributors. The censors demanded extensive cutting of two early films written by Muriel and Sydney, *Daybreak*[46] and *Good Time Girl*,[47] and the much later *Too Young to Love* caused controversy in its sympathetic depiction of a promiscuous teenage girl.

British film-makers of the 1950s were aware that any overt treatment of political issues was discouraged, as it might threaten attendance figures. Box commented that:

> we were expected to produce a programme of films that would interest the general public and encourage people to go to the cinema more frequently . . . We were not engaged

> to indulge our own political or socialist views, however much
> we should have found satisfaction in doing so.[48]

Nonetheless, Box succeeded, to a greater or lesser degree, in inserting her own concerns into many of her films. *Street Corner*, for example, was conceived as a riposte to the highly successful *The Blue Lamp*,[49] which explored policing in London but made no reference to the work done by policewomen. *Street Corner* is intended as a tribute to the work done by female police officers and follows various policewomen as they work undercover, interview suspects, pursue investigations and respond to calls from the public. It is, however, notable that one of the main functions of the policewomen is to restore the family unit: their cases are resolved by the return of an errant wife to her kindly but dull husband and the restoration of a child to his mother, who has re-married.[50] *Too Young to Love*, of which Box was particularly proud, explores the social and psychological reasons behind the sexual activities of the teenage girl, attributing them to a desire to receive and give affection, and to the effects of poverty.

By the late 1950s, Muriel and Sydney had left Gainsborough and were essentially working freelance, making films independently and for various companies. In the absence of any mention of being approached to direct *This Other Eden* in Box's diaries or her autobiography, *Odd Woman Out*,[51] we can only speculate what may have attracted her to the project. Although there were certain of her films about which Box was passionate, she was also an efficient, businesslike director, and she and Sydney were constantly anxious, throughout this period, about acquiring funds for their own projects. On the evidence of her diaries and autobiography, *This Other Eden* was not a film she was passionate about, unlike, for example, *Street Corner* or *The Truth About Women*.[52] Its importance to her seems to have been in the challenge it presented to produce it in such a short space of time, and that it was the first film she directed without any input at all from her husband. It is, however, possible that the character of the independent and outspoken Maire and the exploration of illegitimacy resonated with Box's own concerns. It is also possible that Box knew Emmet Dalton from the time he had worked in the film industry in Britain. In other respects, the project suited her well: a light-hearted comedy in a contemporary setting which contained astute satire.

In keeping with the demand for the Ardmore films to have an international appeal, two, albeit relatively minor, stars were acquired: Audrey Dalton and Leslie Phillips. Although Phillips and Milo O'Shea have since become better-known than Dalton, in the late 1950s Dalton was more prominent an actor than either. Born in Dublin, she had trained in London at the Royal Academy of Dramatic Art and then moved to Hollywood where she worked under contract with Paramount on *The Girls of Pleasure Island*[53] and *Casanova's Big Night*,[54] a Bob Hope vehicle. She co-starred with Alan Ladd in *Drum Beat*,[55] and had roles in *My Cousin Rachel*[56] and *Separate Tables*,[57] both of which were high-profile films, well-received critically and commercially.

Leslie Phillips had, the previous year, appeared in the first of the Carry On films, *Carry On Nurse*,[58] a series in which he was to make frequent appearances. Already, at this early stage, Phillips' image as an upper-class bumbler was in place, having played aristocrats in *Les Girls*[59] and *Just My Luck*,[60] and army officers in *High Flight*[61] and *I Was Monty's Double*.[62] Phillips' neat moustache, fair hair, clipped accent, military bearing and air of bemusement fit well with the mixture of gullibility and determination required of the character of Crispin Brown.

This Other Eden was Milo O'Shea's first significant film role in what was to become a varied career. At the time of the release of *This Other Eden*, O'Shea had only appeared in two films, in very minor parts: an uncredited air raid warden in *Contraband*[63] and a signwriter in *Talk of a Million*, the adaptation of D'Alton's *They Got What They Wanted*. The role he plays in *This Other Eden*, a comic rogue in the tradition of Barry Fitzgerald, is one which he would reprise in films such as

Never Put It in Writing[64] and *Paddy*.[65] Indeed, by 1969 O'Shea's persona as the warm-hearted, garrulous, whimsical Irishman had become established, to the extent that the *Monthly Film Bulletin*'s disparaging review of *Paddy* could write that, 'Milo O'Shea [is] on hand to deliver reams of whimsical blarney over the stout, and it all makes for the kind of folk tale which might appeal to the misty-eyed Irish cab drivers in the Bronx but which Irishmen nearer home will recognize as pure wish-fulfilment'.[66]

Niall MacGinnis is credited alongside Leslie Phillips in the opening credit sequence. MacGinnis would have been relatively well-known to British and Irish cinema-goers, having appeared in several British films set in Ireland in the 1930s and 1940s, such as *Ourselves Alone*,[67] *Mountains o' Mourne*[68] and *Captain Boycott*,[69] and to Irish theatre-goers for his performances in plays at the Gate Theatre. MacGinnis went on to perform in two other Ardmore films, *The Webster Boy* and *The Devil's Agent*.

On 7 January 1959, Box met and auditioned the Abbey actors. Harry Brogan was the only one of the original cast of the play to be cast for the film, in his original role of Clannery, though Ria Mooney, who had produced the first run of the play, was cast as the Mother Superior. Box found none of the Abbey actors suitable for the roles of Conor and Devereaux. Indeed, when she had watched Emmet Dalton's other productions with Abbey actors with a view to casting, she commented that 'they have good character actors, but no stars or juveniles of any worth'.[70] Two days later, Norman Rodway, an actor with the Olympia Theatre, was cast to play Conor and Niall MacGinnis was cast to play Devereaux the following day.

Box received the script for *This Other Eden* on 1 January 1959, eleven days before shooting started. She was dissatisfied with it and her diaries record her continual reworking of the script, even though she is not credited for this. Indeed, in the entry for 31 January, she notes that she worked on the script while shooting continued outside. There was some anxiety about finding a location which would double as the square in Ballymorgan, but on 8 January, it was decided to use Chapelizod, in west central Dublin. The other exteriors were shot at Heuston Station, in the grounds of Ardmore, Glenealy in County Wicklow, and the Wicklow mountains.

The film was shot in just under a month, with cast and crew working long hours, often without a break. In a diary entry for the month of January, Box writes: 'We work ten hours a day and so far extended nights as well, which is slavery to my way of thinking, especially when they want one to include Saturdays also.'[71]

However, the atmosphere on set was pleasant and Box clearly enjoyed the whole experience, exhausting though it undoubtedly was. At the end of February, Box, in low spirits, reminisced in her diary:

> The end of February – v. different from the beginning when I was in Ireland, working so happily, if feverishly, on 'This Other Eden'. For the first time that I can remember I looked around with genuine love and affection for the crew who were working with me and the pleasure which the artists gave me I have not experienced before in films. I was comfortable in my hotel and the only fly in the ointment was the worry over getting the script right, but when that straightened out, I felt carefree, young and vigorous – a sensation foreign to me for nearly 20 years. Maybe the Irish air or the Irish people have something to do with this extraordinary situation, but the fact remains that quite often I had to restrain myself from dancing with joy, especially when I was out on a sunny location day at Glenealy. There was a glory in the air that affected me like champagne, and as I write this I am overcome with nostalgia.[72]

Shooting was finished on 12 February, and post-production took place until mid-April, with Box flying back and forth between Dublin and London to view the rough cut and to supervise editing and dubbing (the music was recorded in Beaconsfield Studios in London, the dialogue at Ardmore). It seems as if there may have been some difficulty in acquiring a distributor – Box notes that it will be a difficult film to sell – but it was shown to a number of distributors in May and was eventually distributed by Regal Films International. Its Irish première was at the Cork Film Festival in September 1959 and it was released in Britain the following month. There are no more entries in Box's diaries concerning *This Other Eden*, except for a brief entry in November, when she mentions having taken her sister Vera to see the film at the Regal cinema in Hammersmith but makes no comment on the film itself.

Overall, Box appears to be have been pleased with the final result, although she does comment on the rough cut of the film that there is 'some overacting by several performers',[73] a fault also noted in the otherwise favourable review of the film in *Kinematograph Weekly*.[74] The film received mixed reviews. For *Kinematograph Weekly*, it was an enjoyable film, its satire softened by its comedy. For the *Monthly Film Bulletin*, however, the film attempted to address too many topics, Crispin was 'a caricature of embarrassing proportions', and the film was saved only by the acting of 'stalwarts' such as Niall MacGinnis and Hilton Edwards.[75]

Both the process and end result of *This Other Eden* show the marks of Box's matter-of-fact, practical style of filming. She reworked what she felt was an initially poor script, dealt with a nervous and relatively inexperienced cast, shot the film efficiently in the limited time that was available and dealt equally efficiently with post-production. The genre, light-hearted comedy, was one with which she was familiar, and the dialogue and pacing is deftly handled. Although Box's directorial style tended towards efficient narration, her films occasionally contain stylistic touches: Harper[76] notes, for example, the sexualization of the *mise-en-scène* in *Subway in the Sky*.[77] The style of *This Other Eden* is generally unremarkable, but the scene of the unveiling of the statue of Carberry, which I discuss in more detail below, is nicely shot, with a clever use of sound–image juxtaposition.

In terms of the themes of the film, in general these are more resonant of D'Alton's concerns than Box's, but the non-judgemental attitude expressed by the film towards sex outside marriage and illegitimacy had been evident in former Box films. She was also a fitting director for a film which raises political issues within a popular format, as the majority of her films touch on potentially sensitive or controversial issues while remaining relatively conventional in form and resolution. As with many of Box's films, *This Other Eden* succeeds in articulating potentially uncomfortable critiques within a comfortably familiar framework.

4

EMBALMING THE NATIONAL BODY

This Other Eden's overarching theme is an exploration of national identity, or rather, of the dominant ideologies underpinning Irish national identity. Through satire, the film attacks those who cling on to rigid notions of Ireland and Irish identity, whether through laziness or for personal benefit. For *This Other Eden*, the ideology of Irish identity as constituted by language, religion and nationalism is a collective fantasy operating in a hegemonic fashion, throwing a smoke-screen over the problems besetting the post-independent nation. The film takes pleasure in holding up to ridicule those who actively collude in the fantasy by forcing them to confront the features of Irish society which give the lie to their ideals: the virtual disappearance of the Irish language, emigration, the fallibility of national heroes and the relative cordiality of Anglo–Irish relations.

The 1950s are generally regarded as a bleak decade, sandwiched between the pride in Irish neutrality that characterized the 1940s and the rapid modernization which occurred in the 1960s. High levels of unemployment, emigration and rural depopulation highlighted the failures of economic nationalism, and the zeal of the Censorship Board continued to enact a policy of cultural isolation. For many writers and cultural critics, Irish isolation, underpinned by the notion of Ireland's uniqueness, had become Irish stagnation. Writers and cultural critics repeatedly attacked the mediocrity of Irish society, what Gerry Smyth, citing Patrick Kavanagh, calls the 'thin society'. And yet, Smyth continues, the rhetoric of an authentic and special Irish identity persisted in the 1950s: 'Radical nationalism [i.e. the construction of national difference] had performed its part in the narrative of decolonization admirably, but now refused to yield the stage.'[78]

Alongside the persistence of national(ist) ideology, however, were signs that Ireland was beginning to emerge from the isolation of the de Valera years. As Minister for Industry, Seán Lemass was putting in place the new economic policies which he would continue to pursue as Taoiseach, an office he took over from de Valera in 1959. Citing the flourishing of amateur drama groups, the emergence of a number of literary journals and the increased openness of the Censorship Board as examples, Terence Brown notes that, in the 1950s:

> There were various signs that a new Ireland, an Ireland less concerned with its own national identity, less antagonistic to outside influence, less absorbed by its own problems to the exclusion of wider issues, was, however embryonically, in the making.[79]

This Other Eden narrates the gradual shift to the new Ireland that Brown describes, its ending pointing optimistically, if cautiously, towards a future characterized by tolerance, honesty and individual freedom and responsibility.

Nonetheless, the première of the film at the Cork Film Festival passed virtually unremarked. Kevin Rockett comments in *Cinema and Ireland*:

> Perhaps *This Other Eden* was made too early and, indeed,
> may have been seen as too cynical even for the new Lemass
> era. It was, of course, the same Cork Film Festival which
> eulogized over *Mise Éire*, the celebratory film of the period
> of the struggle for Independence up to 1918.[80]

There is a certain poignancy in the fact that the mythologized history
that *This Other Eden* critiques was what was embraced by the cinema
audience and critics of the late 1950s. Despite the film's light-hearted
tone and the caution of its resolution, it seems as if the comforts of
the familiar heterodoxies of nationalism were preferable to a demand,
however gentle, to question them.

The Irish Language

Since the inception of the Gaelic League in 1893, the revival of the
Irish language as the spoken language of the majority of the island
was one of the main planks of cultural nationalism. The revivalists'
ideological aim was underscored by the motto of the League, '*Tír gan
teanga, tír gan anam*' (a nation without a language is a nation without
a soul). The Irish language was held to contain within it the essence
of national identity, and only through Irish could the spirit of the
nation be truly and fully expressed, and protected from erasure by
contact with foreign (i.e. English) influence. Although several of the
most prominent members of the revival movement were Protestant
(most notably one of the founders of the Gaelic League, Douglas
Hyde), it was overwhelmingly Catholic in membership and identity.
Thus the protectionist impulse of the revival movement extended to
the perceived need for protection from Protestant England and its
materialist values.[81]

Despite the adoption of the cause of language revival by the Free
State and the inclusion of a clause in the 1937 Constitution stating
that 'The Irish language as the national language is the first official
language,'[82] it was obvious by the 1940s that the cause of language
revival had failed. The numbers of those speaking Irish continued to

decline, especially in Gaeltacht areas. In the 1950s, the revival movement ceased to concentrate on government-sponsored means to revive the language through the schools, and channelled its energies instead into cultural and social projects, the most notable of which was the formation of Gael Linn in 1953. Among Gael Linn's many activities was its sponsorship of two films, *Mise Éire*[83] and *Saoirse?*.[84] Even though, by this stage, the revival movement had ceased to be as dogmatic and conservative as it was in the 1920s and 1930s, these two Irish-language films, recounting Irish history up until 1922, show that Irish was still linked to cultural nationalism, although Lance Pettitt sees *Mise Éire* as 'a cinematic swan-song of nationalism at the end of the 1950s'.[85] Presenting events such as the 1916 rising in heroic, romantic terms, and interspersing its archival footage with shots of nature, the films 'evoke the continuous past of the Irish nation and the eternality of nature and of Ireland'.[86]

In the world of *This Other Eden*, only one individual, Conor, has fluent Irish, a remnant perhaps from the play, where Conor's vision of Ireland is the renewal of its status as the Island of Saints and Scholars. The film satirizes two elements, in particular, of the ideology of the revivalists: the integrity of the Irish language to an authentic national identity and the state's commitment to an Irish-speaking Ireland. Our first sight of Crispin marks him instantly as a near-caricature of upper-class Englishness: fair hair combed neatly from his face, a clipped moustache and an expensive suit. However, the first words he speaks are in Irish, albeit with a strong English accent. His '*go raibh míle maith agat*' to the taxi driver is not understood, and when Crispin explains that it means 'thank you', the taxi driver replies, 'I'm hanged if I knew, and I've lived here all my life!' The vision of an Irish-speaking Irish population is instantly undone by the contrast between the Englishman speaking Irish and the Irishman who cannot understand the simplest phrases in Irish.[87] The film continues this undermining of essentialist national identity when Crispin encounters Maire on the train and confusion ensues as to Maire's nationality. Crispin assumes that Maire is English, because she says that there is not much Irish spoken in Birmingham, where she has come from. Ironically, it is Crispin, the Englishman who speaks Irish, who advocates the Irish-Ireland view: when Maire tells him that he should speak English because he is English, he counters by saying that that is precisely the reason why the Irish should speak Irish.

The issue of who speaks Irish is the cause of further confusion with regard to nationality back in the hotel bar in Ballymorgan. Pat surmises that Crispin must be from Dublin, as he has telephoned to ask if there is much Irish spoken in Ballymorgan. The confusion is rapidly cleared up when Crispin arrives, bidding the group '*céad míle fáilte*' in a pronounced English accent. Pat, showing Crispin to his room, still thinks that Crispin is Irish and, in response to Crispin's questions about the Carberry memorial, assures him that Carberry spoke fluent Irish and hated the English: as Carberry is a national(ist) martyr, the mythology requires that he was also a fervent supporter of the Irish language. In a repetition of the comic device used in the scene of Crispin's arrival at the train station in Dublin, Pat misunderstands a French phrase Crispin utters:

> CRISPIN: *Plus ça change, plus c'est la même chose.*
> PAT: Oh you've lovely Irish on your tongue, sir, and well able to speak it!
> CRISPIN: No, that was French.
> PAT: So it's a Frenchman you are, sir?
> CRISPIN: No, I'm an Anglo-Saxon, or as you Irish would say, a Sassenach.
> PAT: I don't know what kind of a man you are at all, sir, but whatever it is, it's a puzzler!

Politicians and dignitaries are used in the film to expose the gap between the constitutional declaration that Irish is the first and official language of Ireland, and the reality that the lingua franca of

Plate 4.   Clannery and Pat.

the majority, including politicians, is English. During the encounter between Pat and Crispin discussed above, Crispin asks Pat if the speeches for the Carberry commemoration will be in Irish, to which Pat replies, 'Just to begin with, sir. "*Anois, a cháirde go léir*" – that's the way they all begin.' Sure enough, McNeely the politician begins his speech with a few brief phrases in Irish, only to revert quickly to English. By this stage, clearly, the state's support for language revival and its declaration that Irish is the official language of the state amounts to little more than lip-service. The defensive wall of the Irish language that was to keep English at bay has crumbled, not from foreign invasion but from internal apathy and mismanagement. *This Other Eden* shows no regret for the decline of the language, unlike the later yearning for a lost language which characterizes Friel's play, *Translations* (1980), or Bob Quinn's film, *The Bishop's Story*,[88] in which the decline of Irish is expressed metaphorically through the cinematic form of silent cinema. *This Other Eden*'s aim is to point out that, although the cultural nationalist vision, of which the revival of Irish played a vital part, still held sway in the Ireland of the 1950s, it bore little relation to the majority's experience of life in Ireland. The sharper edge of the film comes through its depiction of a people who refuse, consciously or otherwise, to acknowledge that disparity.

Emigration

Though more developed as a theme in the play, emigration is nonetheless a significant strand in the film's condemnation of independent Ireland's failure to live up to its revolutionary ideals. The issue of emigration is imbued with a measure of pathos, highlighting the dislocation of the emigrant, who is never fully 'at home' in Ireland or abroad. However, it refuses to succumb to the romantic notion of emigration as a tragic wrenching from the motherland, seeing it as a choice, albeit a potentially painful one, which can be based on factors other than economic necessity. Indeed, emigration is cast in the film partly as an escape from stifling conformity, and as an experience which broadens the mind.

Levels of emigration had not abated with the acquisition of independence. In the post-war period, the numbers of emigrants rose steadily, though the main destination had now become Britain rather than America. Brown observes that, while emigration in the pre-war period had demonstrated in part a respect for traditions of land inheritance, a means of keeping family plots intact and undivided, evidence shows that, after the war, many of those who left did so because of demoralization and disenchantment with rural life.[89] Thus emigration had become a way of rejecting, rather than respecting, the traditional rural life idealized as the repository of authentic national identity. While emigration had served a useful, if publicly unacknowledged, function in keeping levels of unemployment down, by the 1950s it increasingly functioned to assuage social unrest among those dissatisfied with the monotony of rural life and the conformity demanded by small-town living. Liam de Paor comments that mass emigration 'made a nonsense of the official ideology of the twenty-six county state, of what was taught in the schools and preached from the pulpits and platforms'.[90]

The theme of emigration in *This Other Eden* is explored through Maire, a returning emigrant. In the first encounter between Maire and Crispin on the train to Ballymorgan, Crispin speaks passionately about the wrongs done to the Irish by England: 'We laid upon them the curse of emigration and scattered them throughout the world.' Maire's reply is short and angry: 'I don't agree at all! . . . The Irish will do anything for Ireland but live in it,' thus insisting that Irish emigration is an Irish, not a British, problem, for which Ireland must take responsibility.

Maire's poise and open-mindedness is in marked contrast to virtually every other character in the film apart from Devereaux. These qualities, we can assume, were acquired in part from her experience of emigration to England, allowing her to gain a critical distance from her fellow countrymen and the concerns which exercise them.

This experience, however, is not without a price. In the scene in which Crispin proposes to Maire, she is moved to tears as she attempts to describe to him her feelings about Ballymorgan. Telling Crispin that one of the reasons that she cannot marry him is that she cannot live in Ballymorgan, Crispin asks, with some surprise, 'You're not trying to tell me that you prefer Birmingham?' Maire replies, 'I loathed it. I used to ache to be back in Ballymorgan, even for a day. But even the drab horror of Birmingham could never make me despair like Ballymorgan.' She turns to the mantelpiece to hide her tears and, when Crispin asks her why she is crying, bursts out, 'Isn't it enough to make anyone cry when they can't live at ease in their own country?' Although this speech is very probably one of the overacted scenes that Box was worried about and that *Kinematograph Weekly* criticized in its review, it does serve to foreground why a woman such as Maire would choose the 'drab horror' of Birmingham over her home town.

Plate 5. Crispin proposes to Maire.

In fact, it emerges that the choice to leave Ballymorgan was not Maire's but her father's, who sent her away to prevent her forming a relationship with the illegitimate Conor. For McRoarty, his daughter's emigration is a means to preserve her morality and his social standing in the town. His plan backfires when Maire returns from England and is not only unfazed when she is told of Conor's illegitimacy, but is heedless of her father's threat to choose a suitable husband for her, choosing instead the illegitimate Crispin.

Emigration is presented in *This Other Eden* as evidence of the failure of independent Ireland to create an economic and social climate in which people can live comfortably and have the freedom to express their opinions, rather than being forced to comply with 'decent silences and pious hypocrisies', a phrase used by Maire to criticize the pact of silence around Carberry. It also presents emigration as a means by which the emigrant's eyes can be opened to the restrictions of Irish society, through her experience of another culture. However, rather optimistically, the film seems to suggest that, under certain circumstances, it is possible for the emigrant to reintegrate into Irish society.

The Church

The clergy and the power they exercise is treated more benignly in the film than in the play. Canon Moyle exercises considerable influence in the play, with almost all of the other characters bowing to his opinions. In the film, however, Canon Moyle, played in an understated manner by Hilton Edwards, is imposing, but also kind and intelligent. It is worth considering that Canon Moyle's character underwent this shift in character with a British audience in mind. With a few exceptions, the role of the priest in British films about Ireland is that of peace-keeper, the figure who counsels moderation and, crucially, in films concerned with political resistance or rebellion, rejection of violence. Catholic faith is thus presented as an antidote, or a potential antidote, to nationalist/republican excesses. The play is more specific in delineating this conflict between the representative of the Church, Canon Moyle, and the representative of nationalism, Clannery: the Canon explicitly denounces nationalism as a heresy which induces people to erect false gods. This conflict does not appear in such a specific manner in the film, but, in one brief scene near the beginning, the Canon makes clear his opposition to the erection of a statue of Carberry and refuses to make any speeches at the unveiling ceremony in praise of Carberry.

Although the Canon is clearly an influential figure in Ballymorgan, his authority is undermined in his encounters with the Mother Superior, who wishes to buy Kilcarrig. The comedy of these scenes with the nuns derives from the disparity between the evident wealth they possess and their pleading of poverty, and the disparity between the Mother Superior's forceful character and the lip-service she pays to acceding to the Canon. We have already been warned of the nuns' wealth when Devereaux commented sardonically to McRoarty that,

'The Sisters of Poverty have got a long stocking.' After the nuns have bought Kilcarrig, the Mother Superior enters into negotiations for its sale with Crispin, revealing formidable bargaining skills. But once she has sold Kilcarrig to Crispin for over double what she paid for it, she turns sweetly to the Canon saying, 'Of course, I would never dream of taking any irrevocable step unless it were confirmed by the Canon. Men of his authority are so much more capable than us poor helpless women.' It is principally through these scenes with the nuns, mentioned but not seen in the play, that the Canon's power and standing in Ballymorgan are undermined: he may have influence over the worthies of the town, but he is as putty in the hands of the 'poor benighted sisters'.

The film casts the Church, through the Canon, as a relatively tolerant and flexible institution, encapsulated in the Canon's comment that, 'Mother Church embraces the whole world'. When Conor, at this stage unaware of his illegitimacy, first goes to see the Canon to seek his advice about his desire to become a priest, the Canon does not reject him outright, but tries at first to dissuade him and, when Conor stays firm, recommends that he speak to Devereaux. Towards the end of the film, Conor returns to the Canon, who berates him gently for having blown up the statue, but assures him that, if he has a true vocation, he will be able to partake in church work. The possibility of Conor becoming a priest is not ruled out (in the play, Conor becomes a missionary) but is left open, thus retaining the ultimately benign image of the Church which runs through the film.

However, although the Church and its representative, Canon Moyle, are let off the hook by the film, it is more critical of Church-influenced ideologies, particularly in relation to sexual morality as these are expressed in ordinary people's attitudes and behaviour. Conor's parentage is known to the whole town but has been kept from him, a fact which only Maire and Devereaux express any shame over. Conor's illegitimacy is a source of embarrassment to the town worthies, as it threatens to undermine the heroic image of Carberry

Plate 6. The Canon assures Conor that "Mother Church embraces all".

which is assiduously promoted by them. Conor's arrival the day before the Carberry commemorations provides a source of amusement to the postman and jarvey in Flanagan's pub: 'I'll bet the Carberry Memorial Committee went red around the gills when he walked in! The unveiling of the statue was hardly the appropriate moment for that lad to show up!'

That Catholic morality, particularly in relation to sexual matters, is integral to the ideology of heroic nationalism is consistently foregrounded by the film. The fact of Conor's illegitimacy must never be publicly acknowledged, despite the cost to Conor himself, as this would constitute a stain on Carberry's character: his patriotic martyrdom would be undermined by public knowledge of sexual transgression. The journalist who arrives to investigate the story of the destruction of the statue is well aware of the potential for scandal that Carberry's transgression provides. On his arrival, he instructs the photographer who accompanies him to focus on the part of the

Plate 7. Devereaux accuses Conor of hypocrisy.

inscription on the base of the statue which reads 'in life unsullied'. A horrified McNeely, on learning of the arrival of the press, exclaims, 'Then our shame is exposed to the whole world. We stand naked and disgraced!'

Another light-hearted exchange between Clannery, Crispin and McNeely foregrounds the intertwining of Catholicism and national identity in nationalist ideology. Crispin has dropped the bombshell that he, too, is illegitimate, and proceeds to add insult to injury by revealing that his mother was Irish. Rapid cuts of close-ups of the faces of McRoarty, Clannery and McNeely show their horrified expressions, Clannery and McNeely muttering, 'It's a lie, it can't be possible, no Irish woman would ever . . .'. A gleam of hope then comes into McNeely's eyes, and he leans towards Crispin and asks, 'She was a Protestant?' When Crispin answers in the affirmative, the company is palpably relieved: its cherished belief in the purity of the Catholic Irish woman has not been threatened. McNeely nods with satisfaction: 'Ah yes, that explains it. She was free to do anything she liked.'

Although the Canon is absolved from prejudice, as discussed above, Conor, who wants to become a priest, takes a more orthodox stance on his own illegitimacy. His stated intention in blowing up the statue of his father is to 'destroy the shining legend of a hero that's fraudulent and rotten'. He speaks of his illegitimacy in terms of a shameful taint on his and his parents' characters. When Devereaux mentions Conor's mother, Conor dismisses her contemptuously: 'What was she? Some trollop he [Carberry] picked up in Ballymorgan . . . She was no better than he was.' Having absorbed conventional attitudes towards premarital sex, he is unwilling for the adulation of Carberry and the pact of silence surrounding his, Conor's, true parentage to continue. Although the film sets itself against the self-serving hypocrisy practised by the town, Conor's reasons for exposing Carberry ultimately stem from the same intolerance and lack of empathy. Thus, he is strongly reprimanded by Devereaux in an emotional, highly-charged encounter between them. Conor is still unrelenting after he has learned from Devereaux that his mother was Devereaux's sister, that she sheltered Carberry when he was on the run and that they had intended to marry, but Carberry was shot and Conor's mother died giving birth to him. Devereaux loses patience and comes close to Conor, saying angrily, 'A fine priest you'd have made, preaching love and forgiveness when you haven't got an ounce of human charity in you.' This speech finally gets through to Conor, and he winces painfully listening to Devereaux's diatribe.

What *This Other Eden* criticizes is not so much the institution of the Catholic Church, but the permeation of its ideology into ordinary people's attitudes and the material effect of that ideology on people's lives. Conor's strong faith incorporates an inflexibility and intolerance which he turns against himself and his parents. In learning of his illegitimacy, he is forced to confront and question the values he has hitherto taken for granted. This constitutes one of the film's 'lessons' to its audience of the consequences of a too-rigid sexual morality. Conor's adjustment of his faith to include tolerance and compassion is a hopeful gesture on the film's part towards the future of Catholic Ireland.

Nationalism

Using the device of the visiting Englishman, *This Other Eden* appears to present us with stereotypes of Englishness and Irishness, only to confound our expectations by undermining the differences between English and Irish. It thus forms part of a tradition in Irish drama, and, to a lesser extent, film, of depicting Ireland through an encounter of an Englishman with its people. Plays such as Boucicault's *The Shaughraun* (1874), Shaw's *John Bull's Other Island* (1904), Behan's *The Hostage* (1958) and Friel's *Translations* (1980); films such as Bob Quinn's *Caoineadh Airt Ui Laoghaire*[91] and Neil Jordan's *The Crying Game*,[92] and the television series *The Irish RM*[93] and *Ballykissangel*[94] explore the similarities and differences between English and Irish, frequently casting Anglo–Irish encounters in terms of mutual misunderstanding leading ultimately to friendship and/or romance. The need to explain the 'real' Ireland to the Englishman, to disabuse him of his prejudices or his romantic view of Ireland, not only provides a 'lesson' to the English audience, but also provides an interpretation of Ireland to the Irish audience.[95] Indeed, in *This Other Eden*, it is the Irish characters, as much as the English character, who are in thrall to 'false' notions of Ireland and Irishness.

In keeping with the tradition established by Boucicault, Crispin falls in love with Ireland and with an Irish woman. He is cast as a hibernophile, in love with a romanticized vision of Ireland's past and present. To Crispin, Kilcarrig is 'utterly forlorn, utterly Irish', he is in love with Maire because of 'the music of your Irish voice and your Irish charm' and, in his speech to the angry crowd who think he has destroyed the statue of Carberry, Ireland is 'a semi-paradise set in the silvery sea'. Crispin's imagined Ireland is mockingly revealed as a romantic fantasy by the sardonic comments of the Irish characters, especially Maire, who relentlessly debunks Crispin's flights of fancy.

On the train, she laughingly attributes her success with English men to her Irish accent and realizes that Crispin's attraction to her is part and parcel of his 'infatuation with everything Irish'. When Crispin emerges from the balcony after his speech, flushed with success ('how well they responded to the voice of reason!'), Maire tells him that he is fooling himself, that the crowd was laughing at him: 'You're the best comic turn Ballymorgan has seen in years.' Maire is thus the voice of the 'real' Ireland, her comments foregrounding English romanticization of Ireland as false and misleading.

Although the misunderstandings between Irish and English are initially the cause of comic confusion, the angry reaction of the townsfolk to Crispin's denunciation of the statue reveals the potentially violent consequences of a lack of understanding between the two nations. Even though the statue of Carberry is widely regarded as an ugly eyesore, criticism of it from an English man is misconstrued as a slur on Carberry himself. As Pat says to Crispin, 'You could go around all day blowing up statues of King William or

Plate 8.   The statue of Carberry – "an awful atrocity".

Oliver Cromwell and no-one would say a word to you. But Commandant Carberry, that's a different matter.'

Crispin is accepted in Ballymorgan as long as he remains aloof from the town's affairs, but, once he attempts to become involved, latent hostility against the English is easily roused. Crispin saves himself from attack by presenting his romantic vision of Ireland to the crowd, who embrace it eagerly. Even if Maire is correct in her comment that Crispin's speech is primarily appreciated for its entertainment value, Crispin's acceptance and integration into Ballymorgan is predicated on his promotion of Ireland as a special and unique place: the outsider's romantic construction of Ireland is not, after all, that different from the national self-image.

The aspects of this national self-image cluster around the figure of Jack Carberry, or rather around the various reactions he still provokes in Ballymorgan. Carberry's ghost is ever-present, a constant reminder of Ireland's revolutionary past, a past which, the film reminds us, continues to shape the present but whose ideals have not been lived up to. It is principally through the plot concerning Carberry that the film reveals that Ireland's self-image is created and maintained to avoid having to face up to the realities of Irish life in the 1950s.

In an early scene with Crispin, Pat attributes to Carberry and men like him 'the vast, sweeping changes' that the freedom they fought for has brought. However, when asked by Crispin what changes he has seen, Pat responds, 'Is it me, sir? Oh, divil the change I can see.' In terms of the lives of ordinary people, the acquisition of independence has not led to an improvement. Structurally, social hierarchies remain in place, with the conservative middle classes benefiting from the withdrawal of the colonial power. In this respect, following Fanon, Gerry Smyth remarks upon, 'the coming to hegemony of the nationalist bourgeoisie, that section of the community which effectively hijacks the revolution and comes to dominate, as blatantly as the ousted colonial regime, the post-independence nation'.[96]

Plate 9.   Devereaux accuses McRoarty of exploiting Carberry's memory.

McRoarty, the gombeen man who owns half of Ballymorgan, is an example of the benefits acquired by the middle classes in the years after national independence. Described by D'Alton as 'one of the few Irish industrialists – the kind of man who in former times went to the United States and helped make it what it is' (D'Alton, p. 4), McRoarty's interest in the commemoration of Carberry is limited to the profit he will make from the visitors to Ballymorgan. Devereaux is scathing about McRoarty's hypocrisy and greed: 'You hated him when he was alive and you exploit him now he's dead.'

The investment of the state in preserving an idealized version of the past is evident in the politician, McNeely, who refuses to countenance any perceived slur on Carberry's character. In the scene where the Carberry Commemoration Committee meet in the Canon's office, McNeely's fervently delivered eulogy of Carberry is a humorous amalgam of all of the heterodoxies of nationalism. The eulogy is in response to a question from Sergeant Crilly asking what kind of a man Carberry was:

MCNEELY: Commandant Carberry was a great man, one of the finest Ireland has ever produced . . . He was an Irish patriot, upright, honourable, courageous.

DEVEREAUX: We know all about that, McNeely, what else could he be? What the Sergeant means is, what was he like as a human being?

CRILLY: Could he see the point of a joke, for instance?

McNeely (defensively): What sort of a joke?

CRILLY: Oh I don't mean anything smutty. That's not a matter of humour but of how much you've had to drink.

MCNEELY: Drink never passed Carberry's lips. The gay laugh of a generous spirit came readily to him, and never did it ring out more clearly than when the gap of danger closed around him.

CRILLY: Ah, yes, the dead who died for Ireland. I have you, Mr McNeely. A very solemn thought.

Plate 10. The inscription at the base of Carberry's statue.

DEVEREAUX: You have it, Sergeant, there you have it.
MCNEELY: Have I said a word about him that wasn't true?
DEVEREAUX: Oh devil a word of a lie. You've literally embalmed him in words, man.

For Devereaux, McNeely has stripped Carberry of his complexity as a human being and turned him into a one-dimensional national icon: McNeely has embalmed Carberry in words much as the statue will fix him in stone. The Sergeant's wry response, 'the dead who died for Ireland – a very solemn thought', exposes McNeely's speech as a series of tired clichés which calcify the past and refuse its productive interaction with the present, but which are nonetheless treated with reverence.

Pat Tweedy, representative of the 'ordinary' people, is more perceptive about the myths of heroism and their effect. Recounting the story of Carberry's death with gusto to Crispin – 'and when he was lying wounded be the roadside with gores of blood spouting out of him, wasn't he kicked to death be the boots of a British officer!' – he responds with good humour to Crispin's outburst that the story is untrue: 'But doesn't it make a lovely story, sir, the commandant dying a martyr's death and all.' Pat cares little whether the story of Carberry's martyrdom is true or not: his priority is that it works in terms of narrative and affect. Pat's response highlights the popular response to accounts of Ireland's past and how particular versions of that past, simplified into stirring tales of heroes versus villains, took hold by gripping the national imagination.

The film highlights the disparity between Carberry as national icon and Carberry as a fallible human being in the sequence concerning the unveiling of the statue. McRoarty, the Canon, Clannery and Devereaux are on a platform beside the covered statue, listening to McNeely's speech, when Conor pushes his way through the crowd and stands beside the statue. Cutting between McNeely and shots of the shocked reactions of the men on the platform when they see Conor, the scene moves to a long, side-angle shot of Conor

Plate 11. Conor and McNeely at the unveiling of the statue.

in the foreground, with McNeely clearly visible in the background continuing his speech: 'And above all his virtues was his hatred of shams and lies.' The camera cuts to a medium shot of Conor for McNeely's final words: 'Let it be our prayer that if the hour should ever strike again, it may please God to raise another Carberry for the defence of liberty and justice.'

By juxtaposing McNeely's speech about Carberry with shots of his illegitimate son, the film draws attention to what has been excised from history to preserve the preferred image of Carberry. The men on the platform represent the vested interests of Church, state and capital in colluding in this form of censorship, and Conor's presence, which threatens the ending of that silence, is a reproach to them and the groups they represent.

Indeed, the lengths to which the various characters will go to preserve the 'decent silences and pious hypocrisies' required to sustain the national fantasy of heroism projected onto Carberry indicates the extent of investment in the myth. Even though Devereaux, Clannery,

McNeely and Sergeant Crilly do not always agree, they close ranks when the journalist comes to town to prevent the truth about Carberry and Conor becoming known beyond Ballymorgan. Differences within the community are overcome to protect its public image. While this particular scene is played in comic mode, the film does not shy away from portraying the cost to individuals of manipulating history and erasing that which does not fit: Maire has been sent away by her father for fear she will marry Conor; Devereaux's friendship with Carberry has resulted in his being suspected of his murder, and he has stayed in Ballymorgan, sacrificing more interesting opportunities, to raise and protect Conor. It is Conor, of course, who suffers most, kept in ignorance of who his parents are and possibly debarred from becoming a priest. His determination to tell Ballymorgan whose son he is becomes so threatening that Devereaux actually resorts to violence, punching Conor to prevent him telling the angry crowd that it he was he who blew up the statue.

Plate 12. The angry crowd demands to see Crispin.

Although *This Other Eden* is very different in tone and mode from the majority of films which deal with Anglo–Irish conflict, its treatment of nationalism and violence is similar. Films addressing Anglo–Irish conflict tend to make a moral differentiation between constitutional nationalism and violent nationalism by casting the protagonist as a man (often in the IRA) who has become disillusioned with violence, and the villain as a man of violence who prevents the hero from leaving 'the organization'. The villain is very often responsible for recruiting impressionable young men and leading them along the path of violence, raising the issue of the necessity for responsible (i.e. non-violent) social and implicitly national leadership.[97]

Conforming to this pattern, *This Other Eden* makes a distinction between the honour shown by men like Carberry and Devereaux and the fanaticism of Clannery, who is described by McRoarty as 'a dangerous bloody maniac'. As we see in the prologue, Carberry wants an end to the war and dies in attempting to bring this about. Clannery, on the other hand, is constantly spoiling for a fight, unable to accept that England is no longer the enemy.[98] Clannery's political stance is presented as a knee-jerk, narrow nationalism which has refused to move forward and adjust to the changed relationship between Britain and Ireland. When he hears of Crispin's intention to buy Kilcarrig, Clannery is in a lather of excitement, announcing with righteous indignation that, 'Ballymorgan, the home of Carberry himself, is about to have one of these invading landgrabbers!' Much of the comedy of the film derives from the way in which Crispin inadvertently refuses to conform to the figure of the oppressive Englishman that Clannery desperately wants him to be, but the deeper significance of the humorous encounters between Clannery and Crispin is to foreground the redundancy of Clannery's rabid nationalism. For *This Other Eden*, the English are now the friends of the Irish, willing to admit to and take responsibility for their colonial past and, in the words of Crispin's speech to the crowd, ready to 'work together for the future of Ireland'.[99]

Clannery's fanaticism does, however, have a potentially dangerous side. It is he who is ultimately held responsible for the riot of which Crispin is almost a victim. In his essay 'Images of Violence', John Hill argues that the majority of films dealing with Anglo–Irish conflict fail to invest nationalist/republican violence with political motivation, explaining it instead in terms of fatalism or as the expression of an inherent flaw in the Irish character.[100] This argument holds true with regard to *This Other Eden*: the tendency towards violence is a feature of the lower-class characters, who can quickly transform into an aggressive, angry mob intent upon attacking the English man whom they think has destroyed the statue of the town's hero. However, given that the mob is easily swayed, responsibility for its behaviour lies ultimately with Clannery, who has publicly accused Crispin of causing the explosion. Irresponsible leadership, it is implied, can ignite the latent violence in the Irish peasants.[101]

The comic mode of the film, however, requires that the danger is averted and that Clannery sees the error of his ways, which he does with ill grace:

> He [Crispin] robs, exploits and oppresses us for the better part of seven hundred years, and it's me that has to go down on my two bended knees and apologize to him, and it's him that'll be the hero of the hour! . . . The English come out of everything well: the divil's children have the divil's luck!

Devereaux, who has fought for Irish freedom and is shrewd and intelligent, has the potential for responsible leadership, but his disillusionment with the failure of Ireland to realize the freedom for which he fought has taken its toll. In the play, he is described as:

> an observer of men, who has shed the illusions of his youth, but is still at heart something of an idealist. The bitterness of a man who has witnessed, as he believes, his country fall from grace, the disappointment of his hopes is always with him, but is often mitigated by a philosophic resignation. (D'Alton, p. 6)

It is Devereaux's character which demonstrates the disparity between the ideals of the revolutionary years and the reality of post-independence Ireland. His wry, sardonic comments on the follies of the other characters position him as the film's interpreter of Irish society, creating a detached space from which McRoarty's greed, Clannery's fervour, McNeely's hero-worship and Conor's anger can be observed and critiqued.

Devereaux is alienated from those around him, unable and unwilling to subscribe to the fictions which sustain others. But his cynicism and bitterness prevent him from resisting those fictions successfully. A man who, it is implied, might otherwise have been an active leader in society, Devereaux is now a largely passive observer who, by his very passivity, colludes with the pact of silence engaged in by the whole town. 'I'm the editor of the *Ballymorgan Eagle*', he tells Sergeant Crilly, 'I gave up telling the truth a long time ago.'

The future thus belongs to the younger generation, to Conor, Maire and Crispin. Conor represents the future of a Catholic Church which has learnt the values of tolerance and forgiveness. Maire, who, like Devereaux, is something of an internal exile, need not return to the 'drab horror' of Birmingham. Instead, her marriage to Crispin, an illegitimate Englishman, will enable her to live comfortably in Ireland and shape its future with her intelligence and compassion. Maire stays in Ballymorgan with a man whose English upbringing makes him unaware of the restricting sexual morality of Ballymorgan and its need to maintain a public façade of virtue and patriotism. In Christopher Murray's words, Maire can 'share in English values on Irish soil'.[101] Crispin brings with him a dynamism and an enthusiasm for Ireland, and, though this is only mentioned very briefly by the film, employment for the local people. Crispin's acquisition of Kilcarrig re-establishes the Englishman in the Big House, but this is far from being, as Clannery would wish it, a repetition of history. The ex-colonizer is amicable, sympathetic to Ireland's past and has had to pay handsomely for the privilege of living in Ireland.

Marriage between an English man and an Irish woman to symbolize a cordial unity between the two nations is a device common to much Irish writing and, latterly, films about Ireland.[103] Maire and Crispin's marriage is an imagined, utopian reconciliation between Ireland and England. The marriage between these members of the younger English and Irish generation, who are both a product of and free from the past, symbolizes a future harmony between the two nations that the film wishes to propose, between an Ireland which is free from the twin influences of the Catholic Church and romantic nationalism and a Britain which acknowledges its colonial past and is prepared to enter into an equal partnership with its former colony. The optimism of the film's vision of the future can be attributed to its popular format, which requires strong resolution, to the signs that were emerging that Ireland was gradually moving away from the isolationist policies pursued in the 1930s and 1940s and to its need to appeal to an international audience.

Plate 13. Crispin praises Carberry and Ireland.

Nevertheless, although the film resolves all of the various plot strands, the means by which resolution is achieved are sometimes unconvincing, sometimes contradictory. While some of the issues it raises can be successfully resolved at the level of individual characters, some cannot be so easily contained, and the contradictory and unconvincing aspects of closure are evidence of the 'cracks' in the film as it works to close off the full implications of the critiques it has made. The disjuncture is between the conventional format of the film and the potentially radical critiques it articulates. For example, while one of the main critiques made by the film is the maintenance of 'pious silences and decent hypocrisies', it calls on this very trait to resolve the plot strand concerning Conor's illegitimacy and his destruction of the statue. The community comes together to prevent Conor's connection to Carberry being exposed by the national press: Carberry's 'secret' remains just that, and thus his image of a national hero in the conventional mould remains intact for the wider world, if not for the citizens of Ballymorgan. The film may condemn the construction of a saintly image of heroism which reduces the humanity of those concerned, but, within the form it uses, cannot break the pact of silence it criticizes.

In addition, Maire's acceptance of Crispin's proposal is unconvincing. She had refused him once already, and there is virtually no explanation of why she changes her mind about marrying Crispin and returning to England. The issue of emigration is 'solved' by the marriage, but the awkwardness with which Maire's acceptance of Crispin is handled and the memory of her heartfelt speech to Crispin about how Ballymorgan makes her despair render the resolution weak: emigration, despite the film's efforts, remains a problem which 'overspills' resolution at the level of the individual.

Devereaux's consistent cynicism, however, which is not abated by the close of the film, remains the film's dissenting voice, expressing a continued dissatisfaction with the collective myths which sustain Irish society and underpin Irish identity.

5

THIS OTHER EDEN: THE PLAY

This Other Eden is a fairly faithful adaptation of the play of the same title by Louis D'Alton, first produced by the Abbey players at the Queen's Theatre in June 1953,[104] two years after D'Alton's untimely death from Hodgkin's disease. Extremely popular with audiences, it ran for a record twenty-three weeks, but received mixed reviews. Under the heading 'D'Alton's Best Play', a reviewer in the *Irish Press* commented:

> If one is to accept the picture of this country which he [D'Alton] paints in his 'This Other Eden' which got its première at the Abbey last night, there must not be a cupboard within our four shores which has not its secularly locked up skeleton. But it is far and away the best thing to come from this prolific writer's pen.[105]

The *Irish Independent*'s reviewer was less complimentary. In a review entitled 'Bitterness Mars the Humour of Abbey Play', the unnamed reviewer comments: '"This Other Eden" . . . is described as a comedy; but, though it is funny to the point of farce, the wit is bitter with disillusionment, and it does not really give us the opportunity it promises of healthy laughter at ourselves.'[106]

It seems, however, that audiences failed to register the bitterness condemned by the *Irish Independent* reviewer. Both reviews note with some irritation that much of the dialogue was drowned out by the gales of laughter emanating from the audience. Ciara O'Farrell claims that, as D'Alton's career progressed, he became more and more disillusioned by audiences focusing only on the comic aspect of his plays, refusing, whether consciously or not, to recognize the challenges they made to the complacencies of contemporary

Ireland.[107] D'Alton's cynicism is particularly evident in his final two plays, *This Other Eden* and *Cafflin' Johnny*, both of which attack the preference for comfortable and comforting fantasies over an acknowledgement of reality. As Gerry Smyth comments:

> In every form and at every opportunity Irish writers were weighing the achievement of . . . post-Treaty Ireland and generally finding it wanting. At the same time, many writers . . . were caught between their alienation from, and their commitment to, the new Ireland.[108]

In *This Other Eden*, 'alienation from and commitment to the new Ireland' is split and projected onto different characters: Devereaux voicing alienation and the younger generation, Crispin and Conor, especially, voicing commitment to the future. In general, D'Alton's way of dealing with the ambiguous response described by Smyth was

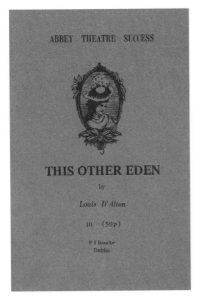

Plate 14. Programme from the play's first run.

Plate 15. The Queen's Theatre, where This Other Eden *was first performed.*

to simultaneously please and attack his audience by presenting his critical assessment of Irish society in forms familiar to and popular with them.

Louis D'Alton was born in Dublin in 1901 into a theatrical family. His parents were actors in fit-up theatre, travelling theatre groups which toured the country performing popular plays, mostly melodramas, in makeshift venues in small towns and villages. D'Alton toured with his parents and was immersed in fit-up life until he began to write plays for the Abbey Theatre in the mid-1930s. His plays fit, broadly speaking, within the conventions of melodrama, are usually set in small rural towns or villages, and several of his consistent character types are drawn from Boucicault, especially the comic rogue.[109] Although his work was very popular, D'Alton has suffered critical neglect, partly because the majority of his Abbey plays were produced in the 1940s, generally considered to be a low period for the Abbey in terms of the artistic standards of its productions. In the 1940s the Abbey was under the management of Ernest Blythe, who, in his determination to promote the Irish language, insisted that the actors could perform in Irish as well as English and significantly increased the number of Irish-language productions. As Christopher Murray comments:

> Laudable as this cultural aim may have been, its effect was to distract from the dramatic responsibility of confronting audiences with the art which questions assumptions and reveals the gods by which people live . . . He [Blythe] did not really care what went on the stage in English so long as it seemed to be fulfilling the theatre's contract, viewed in traditionalist terms. In time, artistic standards fell resoundingly.[110]

Contemporary critics also bemoaned the fact that the Abbey had commercial success as its principal aim. At one level, D'Alton's light-hearted comedies conformed to the Abbey's demand for popular success and several of his plays had record runs, most notably *This Other Eden*. However, the majority of his plays also contain sharp critiques of the mores of Ireland in the 1940s and 1950s. D'Alton attempted to inscribe popular formulas with his own disillusionment with de Valera's Ireland. O'Farrell observes that his method was to use the conventions of melodrama, especially in the first act, and then to subvert audience expectations by developing characters in more complex ways than the stock characters of melodrama, and, occasionally, by refusing to provide strong closure and resolution at the end. This strategy does not appear, however, to have worked with Abbey audiences, who consistently read his plays as pure entertainment, refusing, whether consciously or not, to accept their unsettling elements. *Lover's Meeting* (1941), for example, was conceived as a tragedy but received by its audiences as a comedy.[111]

One of the most persistent features of D'Alton's plays is the foregrounding of the dichotomy between fantasy and reality. In two of his earlier plays, fantasy is used overtly to lend psychological depth to characters. *The Man in the Cloak* (1937), about the poet James

Clarence Mangan, has an expressionist second act, an enactment of Mangan's drug-fuelled dreams, crowded with characters from his past. In *Tomorrow Never Comes* (1939), the ghost of a murder victim appears to his murderer, a product of the murderer's guilty conscience. In subsequent plays, fantasy is incorporated into the realist framework, and its function shifts from psychological insight to social commentary. In a significant number of D'Alton's later plays, including *This Other Eden*, the element of fantasy takes the form of the community's idealization of an individual and its wilful disregard of any factors which contradict the image it clings to with such determination. In *The Spanish Soldier* (1940), a returned veteran of the Spanish Civil War, Kevin McMorna, believes he has witnessed a miracle, and leaves his wife to become a priest. The villagers, with the exception of his brother, Hugh, idolize Kevin's piety, but the play shows the cost of his piety to his wife, Hessy. D'Alton's last play, *Cafflin' Johnny* (1958), which has echoes of Synge's *The Playboy of the Western World* (1907), concerns the eponymous protagonist who returns to his native village to find that, in his absence, he has become a mythical figure, credited with heroic actions in the War of Independence and the Civil War and with having started the *Playboy* riots at the Abbey. Johnny initially basks in the hero-worship accorded him, but, when it becomes oppressive and he tries to escape the persona constructed for him, he finds he cannot do so, as the community will only accept the version of him that it has created.

We can surmise that, in *Cafflin' Johnny*, D'Alton was developing the theme of hero worship which features in *This Other Eden*, his previous play. In *This Other Eden*, the image of the dead Carberry is fixed and ultimately remains so, despite the ruptures caused by Conor's knowledge of his illegitimacy. In *Cafflin' Johnny*, the same process occurs, but in a more sinister fashion, as the idealized object is alive, trapped within a constructed image from which he is unable to escape.

In *Lover's Meeting* and *The Devil a Saint Would Be* (1951), the nonconformist fantasies of individuals result in their being declared insane and pitied by their communities. In *Lover's Meeting*, Hannie lives in misguided hope that her husband, whom she married for love, will return to her. Although she is mocked and pitied, her ability to express her desires and emotions, in marked contrast to the other characters, ensures that she escapes their misery. In the latter play, Stacey's conversations with the Saint, who advises her to give away her money and property, lead to her incarceration in an asylum, but she, like Hannie, is happier than the grasping and censorious characters who surround her. The obstinate clinging to a rigid, impossible fantasy of respectability and decency is the subject of *The Mousetrap* (1941), which was never performed, and *The Money Doesn't Matter*. The former critiques desire for respectability and conformity by contrasting two families, the Hartnetts and the Whalens. The Hartnetts, ruled by an overbearing father, pride themselves on their standing within the community and despise their easy-going neighbours, the Whalens. However, it is the Hartnetts' daughter who becomes pregnant by a married man, and their pride prevents them from recognizing her anguish. A similar critique is mounted by *The Money Doesn't Matter*, where Tom Mannion relentlessly promotes what he sees as the superior social standing of his family, despite his children's failure to fulfil the plans he has for them.

Thus, for D'Alton, fantasy is a double-edged sword: it can be a liberating escape from the dull monotony of everyday life in provincial Ireland, but it can also be a means to enforce conformity to the collective and a means of ignoring reality and thus the need for change. Nonetheless, as O'Farrell notes, the choice is stark: 'to accept [society's] restrictions and be accepted, or to renounce its limitations and be exiled'.[112] In *This Other Eden*, the fantasy constructed around Carberry is one which requires the complicity of the whole community if it is to be sustained. Those who attempt to resist the fantasy are silenced: both Devereaux and Conor are prevented from asserting their views on Carberry. In the play, Conor's choice to remain in Ballymorgan horrifies McNeely, Clannery and McRoarty, and they remind him that they will be morally obliged to condemn him publicly, even if privately they wish him no ill will. Faced with the stark choice described above, Conor ultimately chooses exile.

Another consistent theme in D'Alton's work is the suffering women endure because of the rigid moral conservatism of Catholic Ireland and because of men's self-importance, a theme which draws on O'Casey's work. Tressa of *The Mousetrap* discovers that she is pregnant at the same time that she discovers her lover is married, and the play ends with her dying in labour and her brother being arrested for the murder of her lover. In *The Man in the Cloak*, Mangan is so steeped in self-pity that he fails to notice that his sweetheart is dying – in this respect he replicates the behaviour of the father he abhors, whose own self-pity is indulged in at the cost of his long-suffering wife. In *The Spanish Soldier*, Hessy is left alone and bitter when her husband Kevin abandons her to join the priesthood, having refused to consummate the marriage to retain his purity. *Lover's Meeting* is the most extended exploration of the effects of choosing safe conformity over desire through its critique of arranged marriages. Jane, having had an illegitimate child, Mary, by her lover, marries an older man whom she does not love and impresses upon her daughter the dangers of passion, arranging for her to marry an unattractive widower, as she herself had done. When Mary and the son of Jane's former lover fall in love, the truth is revealed and Mary, grief-stricken, commits suicide. D'Alton had an altercation with the Abbey producers, who wanted Mary's suicide to be interpreted as an act of insanity. D'Alton insisted, however, that Mary's suicide be portrayed as a sane, if despairing, response to her situation.[113] Jane's repression of her 'sin' has disastrous consequences for the next generation, the effects of the past spilling into and souring the present. Murray comments that, 'It is as if D'Alton were asserting that all the protectionism and stress on moral conformity in de Valera's Ireland were but so many pretences when the power of passion is acknowledged.'[114]

D'Alton's work as whole took issue with what he saw as the narrowness of the Ireland of the 1940s, its moral conservatism, religious piety, veneration of the past and mythologizing of nationalist martyrs. His audiences' failure to grasp this critique can be attributed to an unwillingness to be challenged, but also to the popular format through which these critiques were presented, which allowed audiences to embrace what was familiar and comforting and to ignore the critical aspects of the plays. D'Alton would no doubt have been disappointed, but not surprised, that the film version of his play was ignored in favour of *Mise Éire*'s mythical treatment of a heroic past – the precise aspect of Irish society his play took to task.

It is interesting to note the parallels between Muriel Box and Louis D'Alton. Both were playwrights who had a finely tuned sense of popular public taste, Box through her work for amateur theatre groups, D'Alton through the fit-up scene. Each brought this instinct for the popular to their later work, Box in her films and D'Alton in his Abbey plays. Alongside this feel for the popular, both held strong political views and attempted to inscribe them into popular, generic formulas, even if those political nuances went largely unnoticed by contemporary audiences. Both did the bulk of their work in institutions which were in decline from a period of critical acclaim and were driven by audience popularity. The 1940s is considered to be one of the high points of British cinema, declining into the mediocrity of the 1950s, when audience popularity and commercial success were the overriding criteria for a film's success. The Abbey Theatre was similarly considered, by the 1940s, to have fallen from the high standards of the previous decades, its plays increasingly pandering to popular taste.

6

FROM PLAY TO FILM

The filmic adaptation of D'Alton's play is, by and large, one which is very faithful to the original text. The film retains the three-act structure of the play: the introduction of characters and the main storylines, development of storylines leading to a climax and resolution of the plot strands. All of the main characters of the play are in the film, the various plot strands are, with some minor variations, kept intact and most of the dialogue of the film is original dialogue from the play.

Invariably, however, there are changes which have occurred in the transition from stage to screen. In the play, all of the action takes place in a single setting, the Smoke Room of the hotel. The film liberates the action from this one setting, placing characters in a wide variety of locations: the parish house, the town square, the local pub, the newspaper office, the interior of a train and the village streets. The interspersing of characters and their interactions across a range of locations lends the film a dynamism and sense of movement which the play lacks, confined as it is to one location.

However, despite the broadening out of locations, the film occasionally has a rather static quality. A problem facing the scriptwriters must have been that much of the play's dialogue does not provide narrative motivation. While the play's rapid and humorous dialogue maintains audience interest, the audience of a popular film expects narrative economy and a strong forward momentum. One of the ways in which the film attempts to achieve a sense of movement is to inject suspense into the narrative concerning Conor and Carberry's relationship. The prologue depicting Carberry's assassination, which draws on the motifs of the gangster movie (gunshots, screeching tyres, betrayal, death of male comrade), ends with the dying Carberry whispering to Devereaux, 'You'll see to everything – you know what I mean, Devereaux,' thus hinting at a mystery which will be revealed in the course of the film. The hints continue in the scene where Conor enters the hotel bar after his arrival in Ballymorgan. In the play, we already know of Conor's illegitimacy by this stage, and Maire and Crispin are the only characters present when Conor arrives. In the film, Devereaux, Clannery, McRoarty and McNeely are in the hotel bar and are visibly embarrassed when Conor walks in, a reaction observed by a puzzled Conor. The mystery is deepened in two subsequent scenes, the first taken from the play and the second an addition of the film's. In the first of these scenes, the Canon advises Conor that he may not be able to become a priest and encourages him to speak to Devereaux. In the second, Conor overhears gossip about him in the pub, the locals laughing at the thought of Conor arriving in time for the Carberry commemorations. The truth about Carberry and Conor is finally revealed in the film in an emotional confrontation between Conor and Devereaux. In the play, Conor is told that he is Carberry's son as McNeely's speech at the unveiling (which is identical in the play and film) is heard through the window, a device clearly borrowed from O'Casey's *The Plough and the Stars* (1926). In a later scene, included in the film but with much of the dialogue cut, Conor explains why he burned down the Memorial Hall (in the play, a memorial hall is built in Carberry's honour, which Conor burns down):

> I knew I had destroyed a lie. But the lie I destroyed wasn't the lie I thought. It wasn't the lie of a hypocritical Carberry who'd imposed himself on an unsuspecting community; it was the hypocrisy of a community setting up a lie in place of the man that had been, and erecting a memorial to a man who had never existed. The lie I destroyed was your lie, Mr McNeely . . . And yours, Mr Clannery, Mr McRoarty: yours too, Mr Devereaux. (D'Alton, p. 68)

Devereaux, accepting responsibility for having partaken in the 'moral conspiracy' against Conor, comments with grim satisfaction to the others that, 'Carberry's alive again and calling you to account.' (D'Alton, p. 68).

The film renders the accusations voiced in this scene visually in the scene of the unveiling of the statue: by foregrounding Conor it reinserts into the frame what has been excised from Carberry's image, implicitly criticizing those who have constructed Carberry's one-dimensional image. Through Conor, the film implies, Carberry is indeed alive and calling those who have distorted the history of his life to account.

Another means adopted by the film to escape its stage origins is to cut out much of the dialogue from the play in an attempt to integrate these issues more fully into character. For example, Devereaux's speeches about the origins of nationalism and the history of Anglo–Irish relations are excised from the film, as are Conor's visions of an Ireland which has regained its status as the Island of Saints and Scholars and the Canon's warnings about the dangers of dance-halls. While the film's characters are also representatives of particular political positions and ideologies, this is less evident and less overt than in the play.

In addition, there are issues addressed in the play which are excluded from the film. Censorship is one of these issues. The first of D'Alton's two novels, *Rags and Sticks*,[115] set in the world of fit-up theatre, was banned by the Censorship Board, possibly because of its non-judgemental treatment of pregnancy outside of marriage. At the time at which D'Alton was writing *This Other Eden*, the Censorship Board, despite increasingly vociferous criticism of its ethos, was still operating under a policy of 'cultural protectionism'.[116] Despite the appeal mechanism established in 1946, comments Terence Brown, 'It seemed clear that the new body . . . was involved in an effort to insulate the country from the rest of the world rather than in an attempt to protect readers from the grosser forms of pornography.'[117]

Censorship was a means of actively shaping a narrow national identity by a literal exclusion from the nation of ideas deemed alien and corrupting.

D'Alton takes a swipe at censorship in his play, casting it as a practice which limits individual freedom. Maire tells Conor and Crispin, half joking and half in earnest, that she went to England to read a book: 'I was tired of seeing lists of banned books, and I wanted to see what it was the English were allowed to read that I wasn't . . . Since they're allowed to read stacks of things that I'm not, they must be freer than we are. And I object to being less free than others' (D'Alton, pp. 36–37).

Maire also resists more covert forms of censorship, the social pressure exerted on individuals to maintain a silence around certain issues. When she is asked why she intends returning to England, she reduces the assembled company to a shocked silence by her reply:

> because I like the feeling that I can go to the devil in my own
> way if I feel like doing that . . . And because I like the feeling
> of being able to talk to a man, or even half a dozen men,
> without being suspected of wanting to go to bed with them!
> (D'Alton, p. 70)

Her scandalized father attempts to exert his authority, shouting, 'Silence. I tell you. Silence! Silence! Silence!!' (D'Alton, p. 70). It is significant that Maire chooses as a husband an Englishman who does not partake in the collective Irish silence surrounding sexual matters. After Crispin's revelation that he too is illegitimate, he is assured by all present that his secret is safe, but, to everyone's amazement, he asks if he can be exempted from their 'pact of silence' (D'Alton, p. 77). Maire is so delighted by Crispin's revelation and her father's horror that she will be marrying a bastard that she maintains that it is Crispin's announcement which has taught her to love him.

The collusion of Church and State in this covert process of censorship is evident in the co-operation between Canon Moyle and

Sergeant Crilly to ensure that the reasons behind the riot and the burning of the Memorial Hall are not made public. Whereas in the film it is the collective effort of Devereaux, McNeely and Clannery which misleads the journalist and assuages the threat of exposure, in the play the Canon and the Sergeant between them succeed in covering up the incident. Sergeant Crilly simply refuses to acknowledge that a riot has taken place: 'There was nothin' at all happened that I know of. It was the most orderly demonstration of its kind ever known!' (D'Alton, p. 62). As the destruction of the Memorial Hall was, according to the Sergeant, 'a most unfortunate accident' (D'Alton, p. 62), Conor has committed no offence and cannot be charged. The Sergeant reports that the Canon has spoken to the insurance company, ensuring that the hall will not be rebuilt. The Canon has also spoken to the press, with the result that, according to Sergeant Crilly, 'the newspapers . . . are very took up with the desperate crime wave in America. Our little accident will get nothin' but a small paragraph this evening' (D'Alton, p. 63). The forces of Church and State work in tandem to maintain the mythology of a national identity characterized by sexual purity and nationalist heroism.

The play is much more critical than the film of the Catholic Church, a critique which is expressed through demonstrating the considerable power and influence of Canon Moyle. There are no formidable nuns to undermine the authority of the Canon in the play. Described by Devereaux as a Jansenist for whom the only sin is sex, the Canon objects to the Memorial Hall as an inappropriate memorial to a 'begetter of bastards' (D'Alton, p. 59) and because the dances in the hall will provide 'occasions of sin' (D'Alton, p. 26) for the young women of the town. Canon Moyle articulates the ascetic ideals of cultural nationalism and Catholicism. In response to Crispin's declared plan to establish a welfare centre at Kilcarrig, the Canon remarks:

I'm not in favour of pampering the people too much, Mr Crispin. It's too much is being done for them. Things were

> far better in the old days when they did a hard day's work
> for fewer pennies, went to bed at dusk and rose up with the
> dawn. (D'Alton, p. 26)

However, although the Canon's espousal of frugality and the benefits
of hard labour may coincide neatly with the vision of nation
promulgated by the de Valera years, he differs in his objection to
nationalism. For the Canon, nationalism and religious faith cannot
co-exist, as nationalism divides rather than unites the world, and the
reverence of nationalist heroes is 'people glorifying themselves and
makin' a religion of themselves . . . setting up false gods' (D'Alton, p.
24). His speech implies that nationalism constitutes a threat to the
Church because it provides competition.

One of the most interesting aspects of the play, which is
submerged in the film into an undercurrent of Crispin's speech on the
balcony, are the references to Ireland's policy of isolation. In the play,
which is specifically set in 1947, Crispin unambiguously declares his
admiration of Ireland's isolationist policies: 'Let critics say what they
like, but let Ireland persist in her isolation: let her till her own plot
and ignore the world's madhouse' (D'Alton, p. 79).

It becomes clear that Crispin projects onto Ireland a nostalgia for
an idealized *English* past. The empire and the welfare state have
eroded the sovereignty of England and the English subject: 'the
descendants of . . . of Drake and Raleigh [are] standing in queues,
filling in forms, regimented, directed, conscripted. Here [in Ireland]
you have freedom!' (D'Alton, p. 36). Crispin also deplores the empire,
but his condemnation is not based on an aversion to the practices of
imperialism, but rather to the way in which the British empire has
laid England open to 'foreign' immigrants:

> Foreigners of every sort swarmed over the fair face of
> England and blackened it with ugliness and greed, crime and
> disease and misery and poverty. In gaining an empire we left
> ourselves without a country. I who might have been as

English as Shakespeare, am a mere citizen of the
commonwealth. (D'Alton, p. 80)

With England under socialism and inhabited by foreigners, Ireland's
deliberate policy of isolation comes to represent an idealized England
of the past, protected against outsiders and alien influences. This is
made clear in Crispin's speech on the hotel balcony to the angry
crowd below, which paraphrases John of Gaunt's deathbed speech
from *Richard II*:

'This land of dear, dear souls, this dear, dear land.
(Immense cheering)
This . . . er . . . semi paradise set in the silvery sea. Against
infection and the hand of war.
(Incredible enthusiasm)
This blessed plot, this realm, this earth, this . . .' (D'Alton,
p. 53)

Crispin's imagined Ireland is a projection of what England lacks, but
he inhabits this fantasy quite happily, declaring that Ireland is the only
place 'where an Englishman can really feel at home' (D'Alton, p. 26).
The irony, of course, is that the Irish characters, far from enjoying
the freedom Crispin attributes to them, are either busily deceiving
themselves that they are free, to avoid acknowledging that they are
hemmed in by the ideology of isolation that Crispin extols, or they
escape to England to avail of its freedoms. As Devereaux puts it, 'The
Land of Promise seems to be always where the other fella is living'
(D'Alton, p. 27).

In the film, Crispin is the son of the English officer who had
intended negotiating a truce with Carberry, whereas, in the play,
Crispin (now called Roger Crispin) is the actual officer. Crispin and
Devereaux are contemporaries, two veterans from either side of the
war, both men who acted honourably but who have since been
dogged by suspicion that they were responsible for Carberry's death.

In terms of the portrayal of the relationship between past and present, and between Ireland and England, this is a significant alteration. The film effects a more radical break between past and present, placing the future of the nation directly into the hands of a younger generation which is not trapped by the past. In D'Alton's play, the relationship between past and present is perceived more in terms of a continuum. In the aftermath of independence, the ex-colonizer and ex-colonized meet again and renegotiate their relationship with one another. These renegotiations are played out through the figure of Carberry, the man who had attempted to end the war by negotiating with the English. Carberry's ghost is laid to rest when the town is forced to confront all aspects of his life and character, not just the aspects which fit into the mythology of the national martyr, and when Crispin, Carberry's honourable opponent, is assimilated into the country in which he had been the enemy.

As with the film, the play's resolution of the issues it raises is occasionally awkward. In terms of the play's ending, the only difference from the film is that Conor does not stay in Ballymorgan. In a reversal of Maire's change of mind, Conor at first declares his intention to stay, then decides to leave after all. The scene where Conor announces his intention to stay in Ballymorgan is a powerful one, containing some of the sharpest barbs at a hypocritical and craven maintenance of an outward show of morality, regardless of the private views of the individual. Recommending to Conor that he should emigrate, McNeely explains to Conor that he does so out of consideration for Conor himself:

> In private none of us would think any the less of you, but in public we should have to show the strongest disapproval of your existence, even. In private we should wish you every success. But if, in fact, you did succeed, your success would constitute a grave scandal to everyone and be a moral outrage . . . you would find it most uncomfortable. (D'Alton, p. 66)

But Conor refuses to be cowed, perceiving accurately the effect that his continued presence in Ballymorgan will have, that he will become a 'walking conscience' (D'Alton, p. 60) to the townsfolk, exposing their hypocrisy. Devereaux is predictably delighted by the terrified reactions to Conor's decision to stay, exclaiming to McNeely, 'Begod, McNally, you'll look sick having your moral conspiracy ruined by the bastard's moral integrity' (D'Alton, p. 60). McNeely, however, is saved from this fate as Conor, without any explanation, decides to leave after all. In the same way that national exposure of Carberry's transgression is threatened but then withdrawn, Conor's unexplained decision to leave is the play's way of avoiding the consequences of his remaining in Ireland. Illegitimacy is 'solved' by Crispin's revelation that he is unashamed of his illegitimacy and his polite refusal to maintain silence about it. However, as Crispin is English, Protestant and not the son of a national hero, his illegitimacy is not the scandal that Conor's is. The play threatens the audience with the dangerous thrill of the exposure of the national trait of hypocrisy, but ultimately does not carry through its threat.

THIS OTHER EDEN AND JOHN BULL'S OTHER ISLAND

In Shaw's *John Bull's Other Island*, the cynical Irishman, Larry Doyle, predicts a pessimistic future for Ireland, where land ownership will make Irish farmers and landlords as exploitative, if not more so, than their English predecessors, and where the Catholic Church will seek to increase its hold over the minds and actions of the Irish peasant. D'Alton's *This Other Eden* takes the broad structure and themes of Shaw's play, setting the action in an independent Ireland where Larry's predictions have come true. Whereas Shaw's play condemns English exploitation of the Irish, in *This Other Eden* 'that opportunity is reserved for the Irish themselves'.[118] Nevertheless, despite the bitter condemnation of Irish self-deception contained in both plays, *This Other Eden* is, as a whole, more optimistic than *John Bull's Other Island*. This is partly, no doubt, because D'Alton was more concerned with popular acclaim than Shaw, and partly because Shaw's socialist convictions shape his play's construction of an Ireland which is about to be overwhelmed by capitalism. D'Alton also seems more willing to entrust the future to the younger generation, whereas Shaw's future Ireland is in the hands of characters who are either ruthless or passive. *John Bull's Other Island* exposes national images of England and Ireland as invented fantasies projected by each nation onto the other, mobilized for the purpose of gaining material advantage, and it also exposes Irish fantasies of Ireland.[119] D'Alton's play derives much of its comedy from English romantic fantasies about Ireland, but its main target is Ireland's self-construction through the discourses of romantic nationalism.

Forty-odd years later, Shaw's Broadbent has metamorphosed into Roger Crispin. Crispin has Broadbent's bonhomie, his tendency to romanticize Ireland and the Irish and his determination, but he has none of Broadbent's ruthlessness. Broadbent acquires Irish land by foreclosing on a mortgage and evicting the Irish occupant, and then proceeds to give out large loans to farmers in Roscullen in the full knowledge that they will be unable to make the repayments. Crispin's acquisition of Irish land and property, however, is achieved at great cost to himself and advantage to the Irish (in the play, McNeely and McRoarty, in the film, the nuns), who exploit his eagerness to possess Kilcarrig. The colonial situation critiqued by Shaw has now been reversed: the Irish are as adept at exploiting the English as the English had been at exploiting the Irish. Broadbent represents an England which simultaneously romanticizes and oppresses Ireland, and is blithely unaware of the contradiction. In *This Other Eden*, England no longer poses a threat, thus its romanticization of Ireland does not conceal a sinister intent. Indeed, the play ridicules those who persist in imagining that England is hostile towards Ireland, particularly, of course, Clannery, who is even suspicious about England's failure to invade Ireland during the World War II. Broadbent's and Crispin's apparent foolishness masks a determination to get what they want, but, while Broadbent effectively takes over Roscullen by becoming its parliamentary representative, marrying the local heiress and gaining a foothold on local land and property, Crispin is assimilated into Ballymorgan, albeit retaining a position of wealth and prominence. Furthermore, the Irish in *This Other Eden* no longer feel the need to conform to English perceptions of Irishness, as they do in *John Bull's Other Island*. An exasperated Larry explains to Broadbent:

> Don't you know that all this top-o-the-morning and broth-of-a-boy and more-power-to-your-elbow business is got up in England to fool you, like the Albert Hall concerts of Irish music? No Irishman ever talks like that in Ireland, or ever did, or ever will. But when a thoroughly worthless Irishman comes to England, and finds the whole place full of romantic duffers like you, who will let him loaf and drink and sponge and brag as long as he flatters your sense of moral superiority

> by playing the fool and degrading himself and his country,
> he soon learns the antics that take you in.[120]

Maire McRoarty may 'plasther [on] a brogue an inch thick' (D'Alton, p. 14) when speaking to the English, but it is clear that she does so for her own amusement rather than for personal gain. Instead, the Irish have become adept at exploiting each other. To a much greater degree than the film, D'Alton's play draws attention to the machinations of Irish capitalism, represented by McRoarty's poor treatment of his employees. Pat, with unintended irony, comments to Crispin that two of his sons feel that they will live longer and better as flying pilots than as workers in McRoarty's factory. McRoarty and his ilk have filled the gap left by the Broadbents, a fact forecast by Shaw's play in Larry's full partnership with Broadbent in the scheme to turn Roscullen into a leisure park. Larry and Broadbent's plan to charge an entrance fee to the round tower anticipates McRoarty's appropriation of the past, in the form of Carberry's memory, for his own profit.

John Bull's Other Island is unusual, argues Nicholas Grene, in having two 'interpreters' of Ireland, Larry and Keegan, the interpretative function shifting from the former to the latter during the course of the play.[121] Shaw's play is aimed equally at Irish and British audiences and Larry's initial role is to expose to the English their view of Ireland as a self-serving fantasy, and then to expose Irish fictions of Ireland to the Irish themselves. Larry's critical and despairing detachment from Ireland is present in Devereaux, who also persists in debunking the imaginary Irelands of both the English and the Irish. Aspects of Larry's character and its function are also evident in Maire, who also returns from England and, like Larry, perceives it as a country which offers more freedom than Ireland. However, while Larry enters into an exploitative venture with Broadbent at the end of *John Bull's Other Island*, his counterparts in *This Other Eden* retain their integrity. Maire, who has Larry's dry wit, has a self-possession and compassion he lacks, and Devereaux's cynicism never becomes cruel, as Larry's does. Larry, faced with the choice of allying with the muddled and ineffective Irish or the good-humoured, ruthless Englishman, opts for the latter. Maire, on the other hand, does not face as stark a choice: Ireland may make her despair, but its hypocrisy and self-delusions are made bearable by marriage to Crispin, who is cheerfully unaware of Ireland's faults. Alliance with Crispin provides access to an energy, enthusiasm and optimism which is devoid of any sinister undertone, to the extent that Devereaux can state that 'Ireland will be safe in the hands of the Crispins' (D'Alton, p. 80). Shaw's dystopian vision of an Anglo–Irish alliance is one which combines English efficiency and Irish intelligence in the interest of capitalist greed; D'Alton's more benign but woollier vision is of an alliance between English energy and determination and Irish intelligence which heals old wounds and enables movement towards an amicable and productive future between the two nations.

Keegan, a spoiled priest and spiritual visionary, takes over as interpreter at the point at which Larry throws in his lot with Broadbent. His is the most perceptive and devastating critique of the consequences of Larry and Broadbent's syndicate:

> This poor desolate countryside becomes a busy mint in which we shall all slave to make money for you, with our polytechnic to teach us how to do it efficiently, and our library to fuddle the few imaginations your distilleries will spare, and our repaired Round Tower with admission sixpence . . .[122]

Several of Keegan's more critical comments are paraphrased by Maire and Devereaux in *This Other Eden*, but the character who possesses Keegan's spiritual zeal is Conor, also a thwarted priest. For Keegan, Ireland is a holy site which has been brought low, an island of saints which has become an island of traitors but still has the potential for renewal if its people have faith in themselves rather than material

Plate 16. Crispin and Maire walking up to Kilcarrig.

gain. Keegan's vision of a holy land is echoed by Conor's dream of an Ireland which is the seat of a spiritual renaissance which will encompass the world: 'Out of Ireland will come a great idea that will be for the ultimate salvation of the world. We've come back to the path we were compelled to leave for a while, and to take up our work again' (D'Alton, p. 79).

This vision of an Ireland which transcends its national boundaries is in stark contrast to Crispin's desire for a discreet, self-contained nation, willingly contained within its borders. The visions of Conor and Crispin are mocked by Devereaux, but he gives his blessing to both men. Ireland can entrust herself to Crispin, and Conor, in helping to save the world, may help the world to save Ireland. Even if Ireland has not achieved the freedom that men like Carberry fought for, *This Other Eden* allows for the possibility of Irish salvation, whether material or spiritual, a possibility relentlessly denied by *John Bull's Other Island*, which ends with the inhabitants of Rosscullen put off the land for the purposes of turning it into a theme park, and Keegan co-opted as a quaint tourist attraction.

The most striking and significant difference between *This Other Eden* and *John Bull's Other Island* is the contrasting portrayal of the principal female characters. Shaw's Nora is an unhappy spinster who has waited eighteen years for Larry to return to her. She is described as a 'slight weak woman', whom Broadbent sees as delicate and ethereal, but who, for Larry Doyle, is 'an everyday woman fit only for the eighteenth century, helpless, useless, almost sexless, an invalid without the excuse of disease, an incarnation of everything in Ireland that drove him out of it'.[123] Nora is a lacklustre, underfed Cathleen ni Houlihan, still retaining her love for an Irishman who cannot decide whether he wants her and has not the will to possess her, and she herself has neither the courage nor the spirit to assert herself. She accepts Broadbent's proposal because Larry has shown his indifference to her, and because of her strict sexual morality – she has allowed Broadbent to hold and comfort her when she is upset, and because of this, feels she must marry him. Nora represents an impoverished Ireland, ignorant of the world, broken in spirit but desperately trying to retain some pride, and hampered by an unquestioning adherence to the authority of the Catholic Church.

Maire, by contrast, is self-possessed, shrewd and determined and has knowledge of the world beyond her parish, having lived in England for several years. Significantly, she has escaped the restricting influence of Catholic morality around sexual matters. Initially horrified by the news that Conor is illegitimate, she is so confused by the fact that she is still fond of him that she flees to England, but, by the time of her return to Ballymorgan, she can understand her initial reaction as an inevitable consequence of her upbringing. Indeed, the contrast between Nora and Maire is particularly acute around this issue. Nora agrees to marry a man she doesn't love because of her strict sexual morality, but Maire learns to love Crispin at the moment he announces his pride in his illegitimacy. The contrast is also evident in their attitudes to their social standing. Nora takes pride in being the local heiress and is horrified when Broadbent insists she call on people she sees as her social inferiors to assist his election campaign. Maire, however, takes delight in the fact that her marriage to the illegitimate Crispin is a source of profound embarrassment to her gombeen father.

In *John Bull's Other Island*, Larry makes it brutally clear to Nora that he values Broadbent over her: 'We must be friends, you and I. I don't want his marriage to you to be his divorce from me.'[124] As Elizabeth Butler Cullingford comments:

> Shaw's political motivation for situating homosocial desire at the heart of his play, and of Larry's character, is clear. A supporter of Irish independence, he nevertheless respected the English and advocated a close voluntary relationship between the two nations . . . Only the love between men can adequately symbolise political equality; heterosexual love signifies asymmetries of power between men and women . . . Nora is a national token exchanged between males to guarantee continued mutual support.[125]

The transformation of Nora, 'a Cathleen ní Houlihan gone pallid and limp'[126] who is dominated by a blustering Broadbent, to Maire, who freely enters into a marriage of equals with Crispin, is striking in the change in Irish national autonomy it signals. In its early removal of Conor as a romantic possibility for Maire, *This Other Eden* appears to set up, but then undermines, the familiar use of the romantic triangle to signal political relations. Instead of casting the female character as a passive object of exchange between males, the play and film attribute agency and independence of action and thought to Maire. In a play which proliferates with varying projections of the ideal Ireland, Maire is the play's projection of the ideal Ireland, characterized by tolerance, compassion, self-knowledge and, significantly, a self-possession indicated by independence of thought, freedom of expression and a faith in its own moral judgements.

CONCLUSION

In tracing the genealogy of *This Other Eden*, from *John Bull's Other Island* to D'Alton's play to Box's Ardmore film, one can observe the reworking of its predecessor that each text undertakes to modify and re-create its own image of the Ireland of its time. Each of these images is, of course, shaped by factors such as the target audience of the text, the personal interests of the authors and the social and economic contexts in which they worked, as well as the historical period in which the texts were produced.

The clearest change that each text undergoes is the gradual diffusion of the bitterness invested in the condemnation of Irish self-delusion. Shaw's satire portrays the Irish as a pathetic, servile people, trapped by their self-image as much as by the colonizer's image of them, which they can at least manipulate to their advantage on occasion. The only characters who possess the intelligence to perceive this, Larry and Keegan, lack the will or ability to resist it successfully. D'Alton's play retains this bitterness in Devereaux, a disillusioned nationalist like Larry, but one who stayed 'to build the new Ireland' only to see its people 'hugging to themselves a yoke that no conqueror could ever have dared to put on them' (D'Alton, p. 79). But D'Alton transforms the passive Nora into the assertive Maire, who shares Devereaux's cynicism but not his disenchantment. The Anglo–Irish alliance in *John Bull's Other Island* results in Ireland's co-optation into efficient and unfeeling capitalism, but in D'Alton's play the alliance between an honourable Englishman and a young, intelligent Irishwoman lays to rest the ghosts of the past and invests faith and energy in the future. That the illegitimate Conor has to leave to protect the reputation of Carberry and Ballymorgan, however, serves as the play's implicit acknowledgement that the ideal Ireland it envisages may take a long time to achieve. Almost a decade later, in Box's Ardmore film, Devereaux is still cynical, but his analyses of contemporary Ireland are removed, his sardonic comments confined to direct responses to other characters' foolish utterances. The symbolic marriage is now between two members of the younger generation whose parents fought on opposing sides in the War of Independence, thus effecting a more decisive break with the legacy of the past than D'Alton's text. Conor, illegitimate son of a national hero, is no longer required to leave Ireland; instead the film leaves open the possibility that those excluded by the rigid definitions of Irish identity will have a place in a new, inclusive Ireland.

It is tempting to read these changes as responses to the transition of Ireland from the oppression of imperial domination and a corresponding national schizophrenia to a gradual increase in national self-confidence and an emergence from the insularity of the immediate decades following the acquisition of independence. While there may be some truth in this, once cultural and industrial contexts are taken into account the picture becomes more complex. Shaw, a popular and respected playwright whose plays were attended by British royalty and politicians,[127] was able to avail himself of the relative freedom of working in England that Larry describes with such feeling in *John Bull's Other Island*. D'Alton, however, was writing for the national theatre at a period when its priority was the popular, box-office success of the plays it produced. He was also writing in and about an Ireland which prided itself on its insularity and lack of contact with non-Irish influences. From the experience of reactions to his earlier plays, D'Alton learned to leaven his condemnation of the national self-image with comedy. The commercial pressures on Box were greater again. Films require substantial funding and the funders expect a return on their investment at the box-office; the criteria of Ardmore films was, as we have seen, commercial rather than artistic. Even though the international outlook of Ardmore was of a part with the new economic policies of Lemass which would be a major factor in ushering in the rapid modernization of Ireland in the 1960s and the beginnings of a wider questioning of the ideology of cultural nationalism, it none the less required that its films present an attractive image of Ireland to the non-Irish audience. Shaw's grim projection of a nation subsumed by capitalism, its landscape and history packaged for the tourist, seems to predict what his play's textual antecedents grapple with.

If, however, we place the film in yet another context, the history of the representation of Ireland in cinema, *This Other Eden*'s relevance as a film becomes evident. Prior to its release, the vast majority of films about Ireland presented its landscapes as a spectacle and its people as quaint and fun-loving or violent and dangerous. Gibbons's and Hill's analyses of both of these strands in cinematic Ireland argue that they present Ireland as an essentially pre-modern space, which functions either to facilitate a romantic fantasy of escape from the trials of modernity[128] or to avoid a complex engagement with the history of Anglo–Irish conflict.[129] For all its faults, *This Other Eden* by and large escapes these representations (it is notable for containing virtually no shots of the landscape), portraying Ireland as a country struggling with the transition from a traditional to a modern society and the redefinition of national identity that this transition brings about. In this, for all its cautiousness, the film engages in critical and cultural debates around the nature of national identity taking place at the time. In its treatment of issues such as emigration, the legacy of the past, Anglo–Irish relations, religion and illegitimacy, the film marks a beginning, however tentative, of the critical exploration of Irish society and national identity that would characterize Irish cinema from the 1970s to the present.

CREDITS

Director	Muriel Box
Release year	1959
Production company	Emmet Dalton Productions
Country	Ireland

Cast

Audrey Dalton	Maire McRoarty
Leslie Phillips	Crispin Brown
Niall MacGinnis	Brendan Devereaux
Ria Mooney	The Mother Superior
Harry Brogan	Clannery
Geoffrey Golden	McRoarty
Eddie Golden	Sergeant Crilly
Philip O'Flynn	The postman
Derry Power	The jarvey
Bill Foley	Randall McPherson
Pal Layde	Eamonn, the printer
Micheál O'Briain	1st railway porter
Paul Farrell	T. D. McNeely
Hilton Edwards	Canon Moyle
Norman Rodway	Conor Heaphy
Milo O'Shea	Pat Tweedy
Gerald Sullivan	Jack Carberry
Isobel Couser	Mrs O'Flaherty
Fay Sargent	The canon's housekeeper
Seamus Kavanagh	The station master
Marie Conmee	Sister Katherine
Peadar Lamb	Devereaux as a young man
Paddy Long	2nd railway porter
Mick Eustace	Dining-car waiter
Peter Murray	1st Black and Tan
Martin Crosbie	2nd Black and Tan

Credits

Muriel Box	Director
Alec C. Snowden	Producer
Ronald C. Liles	Production supervisor
Silin O'Rourke	[Production secretary]

Geoffrey Haine	Assistant director
Richard F. Dalton	[2nd assistant director]
Patrick O'Shaughnessy	[3rd assistant director]
Phyllis Crocker	Continuity
Patrick Kirwan	Script
Blanaid Irvine	Script
Louis D'Alton	Original play
Gerald Gibbs	Photography
Alan Hume	Camera operator
Peter Tabori	Focus puller
Stuart Hetherington	[Clapper loader]
Ray Mortell	[Assistant editor]
Roy Byrne	[Stills]
Henry Richardson	Editor
Tony Inglis	Art director
Conor Devlin	[Draughtsman]
Eileen Long	[Wardrobe mistress]
Phil Leakey	Make-up
Mabel Ross	Hairstyles
Peter Hatch	Credit typography
Lambert Williamson	Composer and conductor
	Music by Sinfonia of London
Bill Bulkley	Sound recording
Peter T. Davies	Sound recording
Alastair McIntyre	Sound editor
Ardmore Studios	Studio
Running time	85 minutes
Field length	7,650 ft or 2,333 m.
Colour code	Black/white

Notes

1 Muriel Box (dir.), *This Other Eden* (Ireland: Emmet Dalton Productions, 1959).

2 Acting on the assumption that many readers will be unfamiliar with both the play and the film, I have provided a detailed synopsis of the film, and quote liberally from both texts.

3 Henry Cass (dir.), *Professor Tim* (Ireland: Emmet Dalton Productions, 1957).

4 Henry Cass (dir.), *Boyd's Shop* (Ireland: Emmet Dalton Productions, 1960). There seems to be confusion around the release date of the film. Rockett surmises that it may have been released in Ireland in 1957 or 1958. Kevin Rockett, 'History, Politics and Irish Cinema', in *Cinema and Ireland*, eds. Kevin Rockett, John Hill and Luke Gibbons (Syracuse, New York: Syracuse University Press, 1988), pp. 100–101.

5 Fielder Cook (dir.), *Home is the Hero* (Ireland: Emmet Dalton/RKO, 1959).

6 Noel Moran, 'Abbey Cast on TV', *Sunday Independent* (6 January 1957), p. 11.

7 Julia Monks, 'Eleven Abbey Plays for New Irish Film Studio', *Irish Press* (29 January 1958), p. 4.

8 Monks, p. 4.

9 Rockett, pp. 100–101.

10 Monks, p. 4.

11 Rockett, p. 100.

12 Rockett, p. 101.

13 Fergus Linehan, 'Ardmore and the Irish Film Industry', *Irish Times* (13 July 1973), p. 12.

14 George Pollock (dir.), *Sally's Irish Rogue* (Ireland: Emmet Dalton Productions, 1958).

15 George Pollock (dir.), *The Big Birthday* (Ireland: Emmet Dalton Productions, 1959).

16 Don Chaffey (dir.), *Lies My Father Told Me* (Ireland: Emmet Dalton Productions, 1960).

17 Don Chaffey (dir.), *The Webster Boy* (Ireland: Emmet Dalton Productions, 1961).

18 John Paddy Carstairs (dir.), *The Devil's Agent* (Ireland: Constantin/Criterion, 1962).

19 John Paddy Carstairs (dir.), *Talk of Million* (Great Britain: Associated British, 1951).

20   Ciara O'Farrell, 'A Playwright's Journey: a Critical Biography of Louis D'Alton' (PhD thesis, University College Dublin, 1998), pp. 191–192.

21   Rockett, p. 109.

22   Tim Pat Coogan, *Michael Collins* (London: Arrow Books, 1990), p. xiii.

23   Coogan, pp. 400–408; John M. Feehan, *The Shooting of Michael Collins: Murder or Accident?* (Dublin: Mercier Press, 1981), pp. 53–55; Margery Forester, *Michael Collins: the Lost Leader* (London: Sidgwick and Jackson, 1971), pp. 332–334.

24   Coogan, p. 410; Forester, p. 337.

25   Quoted in Feehan, p. 69.

26   Coogan, p. 417.

27   Muriel Box Diaries, 25 February 1959.

28   Rockett, p. 110.

29   The shift from the Civil War to the War of Independence, and thus from conflict between the Irish to conflict between the British and the Irish, is in keeping with the film's promotion of the need for goodwill to overcome hostility between the English and the Irish.

30   In an extant version of the script of *This Other Eden* in the British Film Institute, Devereaux says an act of contrition to the dying Carberry.

31   Rex Taylor, *Michael Collins* (London: Hutchinson, 1958).

32   Muriel Box Diaries, 31 January 1959.

33   Rockett, p. 109.

34   *Sight and Sound*, Vol. 27, No. 6 (Autumn 1958), p. 291.

35   Sue Harper, *Women in British Cinema: Mad, Bad and Dangerous to Know* (New York/London: Continuum, 2000), p. 193.

36   Brian MacFarlane, *An Autobiography of British Cinema* (London: Methuen, 1997), p. 92.

37   MacFarlane, p. 91.

38   Caroline Mertz, 'The Tension of Genre: Wendy Toye and Muriel Box', *Film Criticism*, Vol. 16, Nos. 1–2 (Fall/Winter 1991–92), p. 87.

39   Robert Murphy, 'Gainsborough after Balcon', in *Gainsborough Pictures*, ed. Pam Cook (London/Washington: Cassell, 1997), p. 151.

40   Compton Bennett (dir.), *The Seventh Veil* (Great Britain: Ortus Films, 1945).

41   Muriel Box and Bernard Knowles (dirs.), *The Lost People* (Great Britain: Gainsborough, 1949).

42   Muriel Box (dir.), *Street Corner* (Great Britain: London Independent/Rank/Universal, 1953).

43   Muriel Box (dir.), *Too Young to Love* (Great Britain: Beaconsfield, 1960).

44 Muriel Box (dir.), *Simon and Laura* (Great Britain: Group Film/Rank, 1955).

45 Muriel Box (dir.), *The Happy Family* (Great Britain: London Independent, 1952).

46 Compton Bennett (dir.), *Daybreak* (Great Britain: Rank/Triton, 1948).

47 David MacDonald (dir.), *Good Time Girl* (Great Britain: Rank, 1947).

48 Quoted in Mertz, p. 90.

49 Basil Deardon (dir.), *The Blue Lamp* (Great Britain: Ealing, 1949).

50 Harper, p. 194.

51 Muriel Box, *Odd Woman Out* (London: Leslie Frewin, 1974).

52 Muriel Box (dir.), *The Truth About Women* (Great Britain: British Lion Film Corporation, 1958).

53 Alvin Ganzer and F. Hugh Herbert (dirs.), *The Girls of Pleasure Island* (USA: Paramount, 1953).

54 Norman Z. McLeod (dir.), *Casanova's Big Night* (USA: Paramount, 1954).

55 Delmer Daves (dir.), *Drum Beat* (USA: Jaguar/Warner Bros., 1954).

56 Henry Koster (dir.), *My Cousin Rachel* (USA: Twentieth Century Fox, 1952).

57 Delbert Mann (dir.), *Separate Tables* (USA: Hecht, Hill & Lancaster, 1958).

58 Gerald Thomas (dir.), *Carry On Nurse* (Great Britain: Anglo-Amalgamated, 1958).

59 George Cukor (dir.), *Les Girls* (USA: MGM, 1957).

60 John Paddy Carstairs (dir.), *Just My Luck* (Great Britain: Associated British Films/Rank, 1957).

61 John Gilling (dir.), *High Flight* (Great Britain: Columbia/Warwick, 1956).

62 John Guillermin (dir.), *I Was Monty's Double* (Great Britain: Associated British Picture Corporation, 1958).

63 Michael Powell (dir.), *Contraband* (Great Britain: British National Film, 1940).

64 Andrew Stone (dir.), *Never Put it In Writing* (Great Britain: Seven Arts, 1963).

65 Daniel Haller (dir.), *Paddy* (Ireland: Dun Laoghaire, 1969).

66 *Monthly Film Bulletin* (February 1970), p. 57.

67 Brian Desmond Hurst (dir.), *Ourselves Alone* (Great Britain: British International Pictures/Gaumont, 1936).

68 Harry Hughes (dir.), *Mountains o' Mourne* (Great Britain: Butchers/Rembrandt Films, 1938).

69   Frank Launder (dir.), *Captain Boycott* (Great Britain: Individual Pictures/Rank, 1947).

70   Muriel Box Diaries, 1 January 1959.

71   Muriel Box Diaries, undated entry.

72   Muriel Box Diaries, undated entry.

73   Muriel Box Diaries, 23 February 1959.

74   *Kinematograph Weekly*, No. 2708 (27 August 1959), p. 28.

75   *Monthly Film Bulletin*, (October 1959), p. 140.

76   Harper, pp. 195–196.

77   Muriel Box (dir.), *Subway in the Sky* (Great Britain: Orbit Productions, 1959).

78   Gerry Smyth, *Decolonisation and Criticism: the Construction of Irish Literature* (London: Pluto, 1998), p. 162.

79   Terence Brown, *Ireland: a Social and Cultural History 1922–1985* (London: Fontana, 1985), p. 225–226.

80   Rockett, p. 110.

81   Philip O'Leary, *The Prose Literature of the Gaelic Revival: Ideology and Innovation* (Pennsylvania: Pennsylvania State University Press, 1994).

82   Article 8, Section 1, *Bunreacht na hÉireann/Constitution of Ireland* (1937; Dublin: Government Publications Office, 1980), p. 6.

83   George Morrison (dir.), *Mise Éire* (Ireland: Gael-Linn, 1959).

84   George Morrison (dir.), *Saoirse?* (Ireland: Gael-Linn, 1961).

85   Lance Pettitt, *Screening Ireland: Film and Television Representation* (Manchester: Manchester University Press, 2000), p. 81. Rockett discusses the different receptions accorded to *Mise Éire* and *Saoirse?* in terms of the decline in importance of cultural nationalism in shaping national identity: Rockett, pp. 87–88.

86   Rockett, p. 87.

87   In the play, the Sergeant states confidently: 'isn't a foreigner a man speakin' a different language, Mr Clannery, like a Frenchman or a Russian or a man from th' Aran Islands?': Louis D'Alton, *This Other Eden* (Dublin: P. J. Bourke, 1954), p. 12. Hereafter, page numbers will be cited in main text.

88   Bob Quinn (dir.), *The Bishop's Story* (Ireland: Cinegael, 1994).

89   Brown, pp. 183–186.

90   Quoted in Brown, p. 215.

91   Bob Quinn (dir.), *Caoineadh Airt Ui Laoghaire* (Ireland: Cinegael, 1975).

92   Neil Jordan (dir.), *The Crying Game* (Great Britain: British Screen/Film Four International/Eurotrustees/Nippon/Palace, 1992).

93   Roy Ward Baker and Robert Chetwin (dirs.), *The Irish RM* (Great Britain/Ireland: Channel Four/RTÉ/UTV, 1983–1985).

94   Dermot Boyd and N. G. Bristow (dirs.), *Ballykissangel* (Great Britain: BBC/Ballykea/World Productions, 1996–2001).

95   Nicholas Grene, *The Politics of Irish Drama: Plays in Context from Boucicault to Friel* (Cambridge: Cambridge University Press, 1999), pp. 5–50.

96   Smyth, p. 133.

97   I discuss this in more detail in relation to contemporary films about Northern Ireland in 'In the Name of the Family: Masculinity and Fatherhood in Contemporary Northern Irish Films', *Irish Studies Review*, Vol. 9, No. 2 (2001), pp. 203–214.

98   It is surely no coincidence that Harry Brophy, as Clannery, bears a passing resemblance to de Valera, with his long, thin face and small, wire-rimmed spectacles.

99   The IRA border campaign had been ongoing since 1952, but this does not seem to have much impact on either the play or the film. Tim Pat Coogan remarks that, in general, the campaign was greeted with indifference by people in the Republic, who were 'inclined to think of it as "the IRA at it again" without any clear appreciation of why it should have been at it again': Tim Pat Coogan, *The IRA* (London: Harper Collins, rev. ed. 1995), p. 304.

100   John Hill, 'Images of Violence', in *Cinema and Ireland*, eds. Kevin Rockett, John Hill and Luke Gibbons (Syracuse, New York: Syracuse University Press, 1988).

101   Other films depicting violent, unruly mobs include *Captain Boycott*, *Hungry Hill* (Brian Desmond Hurst [dir.], Great Britain: Rank, 1947) and *Ryan's Daughter*.

102   Christopher Murray, *Twentieth Century Irish Drama: Mirror Up to Nation* (Manchester/New York: Manchester University Press, 1997), p. 146.

103   See Gerardine Meaney, 'Landscapes of Desire: Women and Ireland on Film', *Women: a Cultural Review*, Vol. 9, No. 43 (1998), pp. 237–251; Elizabeth Butler Cullingford, 'Gender, Sexuality, and Englishness in Modern Irish Drama and Film', in *Gender and Sexuality in Modern Ireland*, eds. Anthony Bradley and Maryann Gialanella Valiulis (Amherst: University of Massachusetts Press, 1997); Fidelma Farley, 'Ireland, the Past and British Cinema: *Ryan's Daughter*', in *Wish You Were Here: the Past and British Cinema*, eds. Claire Monk and Amy Sergeant (London: Routledge, forthcoming) on the use of romance as political allegory in cinema.

104 As a result of the destruction of the Abbey Theatre by a fire in July 1951, the company moved temporarily to the Queen's Theatre.

105 'D'Alton's Best Play', *Irish Press* (2 June 1953), p. 7.

106 'Bitterness Mars Abbey Play', *Irish Independent* (2 June 1953), p. 7.

107 O'Farrell, pp. 8, 165–166, 213–215.

108 Smyth, p. 96.

109 O'Farrell, p. 67.

110 Murray, p. 42.

111 O'Farrell, p. 135; Murray, p. 143.

112 O'Farrell, p. 132.

113 O'Farrell, pp. 128–129.

114 Murray, p. 144.

115 Louis D'Alton, *Rags and Sticks* (London: William Heinemann, 1938).

116 Brown, p. 198.

117 Brown, p. 198.

118 Rockett, p. 108.

119 Declan Kiberd, *Inventing Ireland: the Literature of the Modern Nation* (London: Vintage, 1996).

120 George Bernard Shaw, *John Bull's Other Island* (1907), *The Complete Works of George Bernard Shaw*, (Edinburgh: R. R. Clark, 1931), p. 410.

121 Grene, pp. 22–34.

122 Shaw, p. 450.

123 Shaw, p. 418.

124 Shaw, p. 447.

125 Butler Cullingford, p. 165.

126 Kiberd, p. 57.

127 Kiberd writes that Arthur Balfour, the British Prime Minister, attended four performances of *John Bull's Other Island* and that King Edward VII laughed so much at the performance he attended that he broke his chair: Kiberd, p. 61.

128 Luke Gibbons, 'Romanticism, Realism and Irish Cinema', in *Cinema and Ireland*, eds. Kevin Rockett, John Hill and Luke Gibbons (Syracuse, New York: Syracuse University Press, 1988).

129 Hill, pp. 147–193.

Bibliography

Box, Muriel. *Diaries*, 1958–59 (unpublished).

———. *Odd Woman Out*. London: Leslie Frewin, 1974.

Brown, Terence. *Ireland: a Social and Cultural History 1922–1985*. London: Fontana, 1985.

Bunreacht na hÉireann/Constitution of Ireland (1937). Dublin: Government Publications Office, 1980.

Butler Cullingford, Elizabeth. 'Gender, Sexuality, and Englishness in Modern Irish Drama and Film', in *Gender and Sexuality in Modern Ireland*, eds. Anthony Bradley and Maryann Gialanella Valiulis. Amherst: University of Massachusetts Press, 1997. 159–186.

Coogan, Tim Pat. *The IRA*. London: Harper Collins, rev. ed. 1995.

———. *Michael Collins*. London: Arrow Books, 1990.

D'Alton, Louis. *This Other Eden*. Dublin: P. J. Bourke, 1954.

———. *Rags and Sticks*. London: William Heinemann, 1938.

Farley, Fidelma. 'In the Name of the Family: Masculinity and Fatherhood in Contemporary Northern Irish Films'. *Irish Studies Review*, Vol. 9, No. 2 (2001), pp. 203–214.

———. 'Ireland, the Past and British Cinema: *Ryan's Daughter*', in *Wish You Were Here: the Past and British Cinema*, eds. Amy Sargent and Claire Monks. London: Routledge, forthcoming.

Feehan, John M. *The Shooting of Michael Collins: Murder or Accident?* Dublin: Mercier Press, 1981.

Forester, Margery. *Michael Collins: the Lost Leader*. London: Sidgwick and Jackson, 1971.

Gibbons, Luke. 'Romanticism, Realism and Irish Cinema', in *Cinema and Ireland*, Kevin Rockett, John Hill and Luke Gibbons. Syracuse, New York: Syracuse University Press, 1988. 194–257.

Grene, Nicholas. *The Politics of Irish Drama: Plays in Context from Boucicault to Friel*. Cambridge: Cambridge University Press, 1999.

Harper, Sue. *Women in British Cinema: Mad, Bad and Dangerous to Know*. New York/London: Continuum, 2000.

Hill, John. 'Images of Violence', in *Cinema and Ireland*, eds. Kevin Rockett, John Hill and Luke Gibbons. Syracuse, New York: Syracuse University Press, 1988. 147–193.

Kiberd, Declan. *Inventing Ireland: the Literature of the Modern Nation*. London: Vintage, 1996.

MacFarlane, Brian. *An Autobiography of British Cinema*. London: Methuen, 1997.

Meaney, Gerardine. 'Landscapes of Desire: Women and Ireland on Film'. *Women: a Cultural Review*, Vol. 9, No. 43 (1998): 237–251.

Mertz, Caroline. 'The Tension of Genre: Wendy Toye and Muriel Box'. *Film Criticism*, Vol. 16, Nos. 1–2 (Fall/Winter 1991–92): 84–94.

Murphy, Robert. 'Gainsborough after Balcon', in *Gainsborough Pictures*, ed. Pam Cook. London/Washington: Cassell, 1997. 137–154.

Murray, Christopher. *Twentieth Century Irish Drama: Mirror Up to Nation*. Manchester, New York: Manchester University Press, 1997.

O'Farrell, Ciara. 'A Playwright's Journey: a Critical Biography of Louis D'Alton.' PhD thesis, University College Dublin, 1998.

O'Leary, Philip. *The Prose Literature of the Gaelic Revival: Ideology and Innovation*. Pennsylvania: Pennsylvania State University Press, 1994.

Pettitt, Lance. *Screening Ireland: Film and Television Representation*. Manchester: Manchester University Press, 2000.

Rockett, Kevin. 'History, Politics and Irish Cinema', in *Cinema and Ireland*, eds. Kevin Rockett, John Hill and Luke Gibbons. Syracuse, New York: Syracuse University Press, 1988. 3–145.

Shaw, George Bernard. *The Complete Works of George Bernard Shaw*. Edinburgh: R. & R. Clark, 1931.

Smyth, Gerry. *Decolonisation and Criticism: the Construction of Irish Literature*. London: Pluto, 1998.

Taylor, Rex. *Michael Collins*. London: Hutchinson, 1958.